SALISBURY CATHEDRAL

Salisbury Cathedral from the North-east, *c.* 1940

SALISBURY CATHEDRAL

AN ECCLESIASTICAL HISTORY

by

Kathleen Edwards, M.A., Ph.D., F.S.A.

Reprinted from
THE VICTORIA HISTORY OF WILTSHIRE
VOLUME III
edited by R. B. Pugh and Elizabeth Crittall
and published by
OXFORD UNIVERSITY PRESS
for the
INSTITUTE OF HISTORICAL RESEARCH

WILTSHIRE COUNTY COUNCIL LIBRARY & MUSEUM SERVICE
Trowbridge
1986

ACKNOWLEDGEMENTS AND NOTES

This reprint has been produced as part of the Library & Museum Service's policy of making material on the County more widely available by publishing or republishing items not currently in print. A request from the Dean of Salisbury, the Very Reverend S. H. Evans, to reprint this history of Salisbury Cathedral was therefore welcomed and his support and that of the Institute of Historical Research through the General Editor of the Victoria History, Mr. C. R. Elrington, are gratefully acknowledged, as is the assistance of Dr. D. A. Crowley, Editor of the Victoria History of Wiltshire.

The pagination of the original volume has been retained and references to pages outside this sequence may be seen in the main volume. Although it has not proved possible to reproduce the index to that volume, a list of contents has been added on the page preceding the main text. All the illustrations used appear in the main volume but their position in the text has been altered. The cover illustration is taken from J. M. W. Turner's *The interior of Salisbury Cathedral looking towards the North Transept* which is reproduced by kind permission of Salisbury and South Wiltshire Museum.

Since the publication of the original volume, Salisbury Diocesan records have been transferred to the County Record Office in Trowbridge and the Records Branch of the Wiltshire Archaeological and Natural History Society has become the Wiltshire Record Society.

Printed in Great Britain by Redwood Burn Limited, Trowbridge, Wiltshire
ISBN 0 86080 140 3

CONTENTS

THE CATHEDRAL OF SALISBURY

THE FOUNDATION

The foundation of Salisbury Cathedral Chapter has a special importance in English ecclesiastical history. It formed a part of the Norman reorganization of the English Church, which had far-reaching results. The decision of the Council of London to move the united sees of Sherborne and Ramsbury to Salisbury[1] gave the opportunity for a completely new start in a city where the Normans, unhampered by Anglo-Saxon precedents or vested interests, were able to work out ideas of secular cathedral government new to England. Moreover, the work was carried out with special success by the most distinguished of the Conqueror's curial bishops, St. Osmund, who alone among the Norman bishops left a written constitution for his cathedral chapter. His Institution seems to have been the main source both of the later 'four-square' constitution of the English secular cathedrals of the Old Foundation, based on the four great dignitaries, dean, precentor, chancellor, and treasurer, with their stalls at the four corners of the choir,[2] and of the later prestige of Salisbury chapter. Because of the Institution other English secular chapters naturally turned to Salisbury for constitutional precedents and as the fount of their liberties. By the 14th century this had resulted in a remarkable homogeneity in their constitutions. The early constitutional prestige of Salisbury may also have been partly responsible for the overwhelming victory of the Use of Salisbury in Britain in the later Middle Ages.

The establishment of the chapter, however, took a long time. At Sherborne the cathedral had been served by Benedictine monks since about 993,[3] whilst at Ramsbury there was apparently neither an organized body of clerks nor the resources for maintaining them.[4] The building of the new cathedral was begun during the last three years of the life of Bishop Herman,[5] a foreigner from Flanders, who had ruled Ramsbury since 1045 and the united sees of Sherborne and Ramsbury since 1058. The accession of Osmund in 1078, however, marks the real beginning of the new era at Salisbury. Under him the building of the cathedral was completed. It lay in the north-west quarter of the Saxon town, later known as Old Salisbury, within the new Norman castle on the peak of the high mound.[6] The general plan of the church reflected the most common Norman practice of three apses (i.e. an apsidal east end, and north and south transepts with eastern apses) and solid walls for the choir, but it was apparently not entirely Norman in conception. Excavations have shown that it can never have had provision for a central tower, and that it may have been designed for transeptal towers, which were unknown in Normandy.[7] It was not ready for consecration until 1092, and five days later was struck by lightning and partially destroyed.[8] In the previous year, 1091, according to 15th-century tradition, Bishop Osmund had ordained 4 principal *personae*, 32 prebendaries, 4 archdeacons, a sub-dean, and a succentor, but these arrangements may well have been put into practice a few years before the issue of a formal foundation charter.[9]

The two most important documents in the early history of Salisbury Chapter are St. Osmund's foundation charter, which endowed it, and his Institution which laid down its constitutional arrangements. Unfortunately the original of neither has survived, and the earliest known copies of the Institution date from the early 14th and early 15th centuries.[10] There seems, however, little reason to doubt that both charters in their present form are copies, however far removed, of documents originally drawn up by St. Osmund, and, judging from the later history of the chapter's estates, the copies of the foundation charter at least are substantially accurate. The endowment comprised a generous slice of the episcopal property, unburdened by military service, and mostly within the diocese, with outlying properties in Somerset and Lincolnshire. The Dorset estates, which had originally belonged to the see of Sherborne, were formed from the 5 vills, apart from knights' fees which were retained by the bishop, of Yetminster, Alton Pancras, Charminster, Beaminster, and Netherbury, and the three churches of Sherborne, Bere Regis, and St. George, Fordington, in Dorchester. The Wiltshire property was more extensive, with land in the bishop's vill of Salisbury, in Stratford-sub-Castle, and before the castle gate of Salisbury for the canons' houses and gardens, and 11½ churches, including both Salisbury and

[1] D. Wilkins, *Concilia Magnae Britanniae* (1737), i, 363; Wm. of Malmesbury, *Gest. Pont.* (Rolls Ser.), 67.

[2] Cf. H. Bradshaw and C. Wordsworth, *Linc. Cath. Stat.* (1892), i, 102–3.

[3] M. D. Knowles, *Mon. Order in Engl.* 50.

[4] *Gest. Pont.* (Rolls Ser.), 182.

[5] *D.N.B.* s.v. Hermann; *Gest. Pont.* (Rolls Ser.), 182–3.

[6] *Arch. Jnl.* civ (1947), 127, 140.

[7] A. W. Clapham, *Engl. Romanesque Archit. after the Conquest*, 22, 48, 61; *Arch. Jnl.* civ (1947), 142.

[8] *Gest. Regum* (Rolls Ser.), ii, 375; Simeon of Durham, *Chron.* (Rolls Ser.), ii, 219; Florence of Worcester, *Chron.* (Eng. Hist. Soc.), ii, 30; Roger of Hoveden, *Chron.* (Rolls Ser.), i, 145; *Chron. of Holyrood* (Scottish Hist. Soc.), 111.

[9] *Stat. Sar. Cath.* ed. C. Wordsworth and D. Macleane, 24–25; according to *Chron. of Holyrood*, 110, it was in 1089 that he ordained 36 canons.

[10] The two earliest known copies of the Institution are in the 13th-cent. Reg. of St. Osmund (Sar. Dioc. Regy.), ff. 47–48, in an early 14th-cent. hand, and in Reg. of Canonization of St. Osmund (D. & C. Sar.), 1424–57, ff. 41–43, which is thought to be more accurate. The foundation charter is in the Reg. of St. Osmund, f. 41; in the early 14th-cent. Registrum Rubrum (Sar. Dioc. Regy.), f. 1, and in the Reg. of Canonization of St. Osmund, ff. 38–40. Both have been printed several times: in Hoare, *Mod. Wilts.* Salisbury, 717; *Reg. St. Osmund* (Rolls Ser.), i, 198–200, 212–15; *Linc. Cath. Stat.* ed. H. Bradshaw and C. Wordsworth, ii, 7–10; *Use Sar.* ed. W. H. Frere, i, 257–61; *Canonization S. Osmund*, ed. A. R. Malden (Wilts. Rec. Soc.), 46–52; *Stat. Sar.* 16–35.

Ramsbury, Wilsford near Woodford, Potterne, West Lavington, Bishop's Cannings, Calne, Highworth, Marlborough, Great Bedwyn, Wanborough, with land in Wanborough, and half of Mere church. In Berkshire, which had also belonged to the see of Ramsbury, there were three churches, Great Faringdon, Sonning, and Blewbury, with 10 hides at Ruscombe; in Somerset the vill or manor of Writhlington, except for knights' lands; and, far to the north in Lincolnshire, the two churches of Grantham, which Osmund may have acquired while a royal commissary for the Domesday survey on the midland circuit.[11] In addition Osmund granted to the canons half the offerings on the high altar of the cathedral and all the offerings of the other altars. Two-thirds of a deceased canon's prebend was to be shared by the other canons during the year following his death, the remaining third going to the poor. All this property was given for the souls of King William, Queen Maud, their son William II, and Bishop Osmund. The charter was said to have been sealed in 1091. Among the many witnesses were Archbishop Thomas of York, Bishop Rémy of Lincoln, and Bishop Maurice of London, who were then reorganizing their cathedral chapters on a secular basis.[12]

The same three bishops witnessed St. Osmund's Institution Charter, also of 1091,[13] and all four may have consulted together about their plans. The Institution is a short document, generally clear and succinct, but somewhat confused in dealing with the dignitaries. First, in a preamble, Osmund claimed the advice of his fellow bishops and the assent of the king. Secondly, the rules of residence were set out. The four principal dignitaries, dean, chanter, chancellor, and treasurer, were to be resident assiduously; two archdeacons were always to be resident unless excused by a good reason; the canons might be absent only if attending the schools or in the king's service; the king might employ one canon in his chapel, the archbishop one, and the bishop three; one-third of the year might be spent by a canon on business for the benefit of the church or his prebend. Thirdly, privileges and jurisdiction were granted to the dean and canons. They were to answer to the bishop only in chapter, and obey the chapter's judgement only. They were to have their own court with archidiaconal jurisdiction in all their prebends, and the same liberties and privileges which the bishop had enjoyed in the prebends while they had been in his domain. Fourthly, the liberties and functions of dignitaries, officers, and canons were described, with a few lesser matters. The dean was superior to canons and vicars in the rule of souls and correction of behaviour. The chanter ruled the choir in singing; the treasurer kept the treasures and ornaments and provided the lights; the chancellor ruled the schools and corrected the books; the archdeacons were powerful in the care of parishes and cure of souls. The dean, chanter, treasurer, and chancellor received double commons, the other canons single commons; but only residents might share in the common fund. A canon present at a church's dedication might share the offerings with the bishop's chaplains, but if the bishop dedicated the church or chapel of a prebend the canon of the prebend received all the offerings. The sub-dean held the archdeaconry of the city and suburbs from the dean, and the sub-chanter or succentor received the appurtenances of the chantry from the chanter. The *archiscola* heard the lessons read, decided on their length; kept the church's seal; composed letters, charters, and wrote the readers' names on the board; and the chanter did the same for the singers. Finally, in matters of discipline, the elders were to be besought like brethren, but if they were absent too often without reasonable cause from the daily mass or canonical hours, and did not reform after correction, they were to be punished in chapter, prostrate before the dean and brethren. If guilty of disobedience, rebellion, or other notorious faults, they were to be degraded from their stalls and do penance. If they appeared incorrigible, they were to suffer more severe punishment.

This constitution may have been drawn partly from those of the cathedrals of northern France, of which Bayeux most resembled Salisbury, but probably St. Osmund relied also on experience gained from experiments at Salisbury made during the building of the cathedral, and followed no definite model, trying simply to establish the kind of chapter which he thought would work best.[14] He may also, it has been suggested,[15] have used a written source, the *Tractatus de Officiis Ecclesiasticis* of Bishop John of Avranches, a liturgist and friend of Lanfranc, whose work was promulgated in the 1060's as the official Use of the province of Rouen.

The passages of the Institution dealing with the *archiscola* and chancellor form the main obstacle to belief in the complete accuracy of the existing text. There is no real difficulty in accounting for the use of the title chancellor in 1091. Osmund could have taken it from his own office of royal chancellor, or from Chartres Cathedral, or from the treatise of John of Avranches, while *archiscola* could have been a variant of *magister scholarum* or *scholasticus*, which were then the more usual titles given to the dignitary in charge of the cathedral schools. But there is a somewhat puzzling confusion in Osmund's description of their functions,

[11] Cf. *Fasti Eccl. Sar.* ed. Jones, 40; *D.N.B.* s.v. Osmund.

[12] Cf. K. Edwards, *Eng. Secular Cath. in Middle Ages*, 13–20; C. N. L. Brooke, 'Composition of St. Paul's Chapter, 1086–1163', *Camb. Hist. Jnl.* x (1951), 118–19.

[13] *Martinus* in both copies is probably a scribal error for *Mauricius*. Mauricius, Bp. of London, witnessed the foundation charter: *Stat. Sar.* 22–23.

[14] Cf. Edwards, *Eng. Secular Cath.* 13–19, 259–60, 326–7.

[15] By Mr. C. N. L. Brooke in 'English Cathedral Chapters and the Norman Conquest', an unpublished paper read to the Stubbs Society at Oxford, 1952.

which in the Salisbury Consuetudinary of about 1210 are all attributed to the chancellor.[16] The most likely explanation seems to be that they were the same person described by different titles, and that originally the title *archiscola* was used for the third or fourth dignitary throughout the document.[17] Later in the 12th century, as the secretarial business of the chapter increased, the title chancellor may gradually have displaced *archiscola*, and the Institution have been brought up to date by inserting the title, chancellor, though clumsily, since the *archiscola* was not effectively eliminated. This suggestion is supported by examination of the practice at Salisbury in the first half of the 12th century. Before about 1155 no chancellor has been traced, but there is definite evidence for a *magister scholarum* or *scholiarcha* (evidently a variant of *archiscola*) in 1107 and in 1139.[18] Most other essential provisions of the Institution apparently existed at Salisbury by the early 12th century, which suggests that the rest of the text is substantially genuine, or at least dates from a very early period in the chapter's history. The names of a dean and three archdeacons have been found in Osmund's time.[19] In 1122 the first known list of dignitaries witnessing a charter includes a dean, chanter, treasurer, a *magister Ailwinus* (possibly another master of the schools), an archdeacon, and a sub dean.[20] About the same time commons were being paid for attendance at the cathedral services, and the name of the first known vicar choral is found.[21] Finally, by the mid-12th century a succentor, Roger, appears.[22] There were to be many later modifications of the Institution; its merit was that it was essentially a practical document, which later generations could adapt to their needs.

A few more conclusions may be hazarded about the early chapter. The names of the deans suggest that they were Normans or Frenchmen. Gunter, one of the first known archdeacons, and Master Guy d'Étampes, the first known master of the schools, came from Le Mans (Sarthe).[23] But, in spite of continental connexions, Anglo-Saxon traditions of Christianity in Wessex do not seem to have been rejected or forgotten. St. Osmund took trouble to procure for his cathedral a relic of St. Aldhelm, his predecessor as Bishop of Sherborne 300 years before. Moreover, the list of witnesses to the charter of 1122 in Bishop Roger's time suggests that the chapter was then recruited from Anglo-Saxons as well as Normans and Frenchmen. Five of the twelve names have an obviously Anglo-Saxon origin.[24] Earlier William of Malmesbury wrote that Bishop Osmund 'not only willingly kept clerks distinguished in learning from wherever they came, but generously forced them to remain, so that the fame of the canons in song and learning (*litteratura*) shone forth more nobly there [at Salisbury] than elsewhere. Many books were acquired, and the bishop himself did not disdain to write and bind them'.[25] He is also said to have given many ornaments, jewels, and vestments to his cathedral.[26] His efforts to make his cathedral a centre of study and worship seem to have borne some fruit. The 'Meditations to Rainilva, a recluse' of Godwin, the chanter of 1122, who was later buried at Salisbury, show learning, tolerance, and a spirit of homely piety; other writings, now lost, of a literary and spiritual character, have been attributed to him.[27] Several of the early cathedral clergy entered religion.[28] About 65 books are thought to have survived from the scriptorium.[29] Written on poor parchment, with the simplest decoration, they are not the books of a rich community, and it is tempting to suppose that they were the work of St. Osmund and his canons. No evidence has been found for the later tradition that a Use of Salisbury was composed at this time.[30]

OLD SALISBURY

It is not known how the property given by St. Osmund was first divided or how far it was adequate, but about 28 of the later full number of 52 or 53 medieval prebends seem to have been formed mainly from it, as well as part of the deanery's estates, and a small part of the common fund; quite possibly, therefore, it originally maintained 32 or 36 prebendaries. This property was more than doubled in the 12th and early 13th centuries by gifts from kings, lay magnates, bishops, and as time went on from less

[16] *Use Sar.* i, 3–4.

[17] Edwards, *Eng. Secular Cath.* 184–5.

[18] Ibid. 185; *Sar. Chart. & Doc.* (Rolls Ser.), 8–9.

[19] Walter, the first dean, Gunter of Le Mans, Archd. of Salisbury before 1085: Orderic Vitalis, *Eccl. Hist.* (Soc. de l'hist. de France), iv, 280–2 and n.; Everard and Hubald, archds. by *c.* 1078–81: *Gest. Pont.* (Rolls Ser.), 429–31.

[20] *Reg. St. Osmund* (Rolls Ser.), i, 381, where it is wrongly dated; for 1122 see W. Farrer, *Itin. Hen. I*, no. 474. Godwin, given as chancellor, was in fact cantor: Edwards, *Eng. Secular Cath.* p. 185.

[21] *Sar. Chart. & Doc.* (Rolls Ser.), 16–17.

[22] Hist. MSS. Com. *Var. Coll.* i, 370–1.

[23] Orderic Vitalis, *Hist. Eccl.* (Soc. de l'hist. de France), iv, 282; *Hildeberti Epistolae* (*Patrologia Latina*, clxxi), ed. Migne, c. 219; *Actus Pontificum Cenomannis* (Vetera Analecta), ed. Mabillon, 320.

[24] *Reg. St. Osmund* (Rolls Ser.), i, 381. For the names see O. Von Feilitzen, *Pre-Conquest Names of Dom. Bk.* (Uppsala, 1937).

[25] *Gest. Pont.* (Rolls Ser.), 184.

[26] *Ceremonies and Processions Sar.* ed. C. Wordsworth, 183–4; *Stat. Sar.* 34–39.

[27] Bodl. Digby MS. 96, ff. 20*b*–21*a*; *Proc. Soc. Antiq.* 2nd ser. xxvi (1913–14), 113, plate facing p. 110; H. E. Allen, 'On the Author of the Ancren Riwle', *Pubns. Mod. Lang. Assocn.* xliv (1929), 639–40, 666–9.

[28] e.g. Gunter became a monk at Battle, and Abbot of Thorney in 1085; Serlo, dean in 1122, was probably the Serlo who became Abbot of Cirencester, 1130 or 1131; Robert, a vicar choral *c.* 1122, became Prior of Breamore: Orderic Vitalis, *Hist. Eccl.* (Soc. de l'hist. de France), iv, 280–2 and n.; Florence of Worc. *Chron.* (Eng. Hist. Soc.), ii, 92; Leland, *Itin.* ed. Toulmin Smith, i, 265; *Sar. Chart. & Doc.* (Rolls Ser.), 16–17.

[29] N. R. Ker, 'Salisbury Cathedral Manuscripts', *W.A.M.* liii, 153–5.

[30] For this tradition: *Linc. Cath. Stat.* ed. H. Bradshaw and C. Wordsworth, iii, 860–88; W. H. Frere, *Use Sar.* i, xvii–xviii.

important clergy and laity. The chapter became a rich and privileged corporation, and particular estates were assigned to particular purposes.

The most spectacular increases in property came in Henry I's reign, doubtless due largely to Bishop Roger's influence at court, as well as to the genuine interest of king and barons in St. Osmund's new foundation. A charter of Henry, probably granted towards the end of his reign, shows that gifts from himself and others to the chapter since 1091 in Wiltshire alone included 12½ churches (Heytesbury, Sutton Benger, Netheravon, Burbage, Britford, Combe Bissett, West Harnham, the other half of Mere, Westbury, Figheldean, Alderbury with its chapels of Farley and Pitton, and Stapleford), and land in Ratfyn, in Amesbury, and Warminster. In addition ten more churches outside the diocese had been granted to it: Godalming (Surr.), Hurstbourne, King's Somborne and Odiham (Hants), Bedminster and Redcliffe (Som.), Alveston (Glos.), Swinbrook and Shipton (Oxon.), and Brixworth (Northants.), the last three, with land at Overcott in Swindon, being given for two prebends by Arnulf the Falconer, a servant of William the Conqueror. Henry also gave the canons freedom from geld and from tolls and customs in markets and fairs throughout England, timber from royal forests for repairing their church, the right to hold an annual fair at Salisbury from 3 to 9 September, and, for their common fund, the tithes of the royal forests in Wiltshire, Hampshire, Dorset, and Berkshire.[31] Other gifts of the reign were the tolls of Salisbury market from Henry's queen, Maud; land and rents from Croc the Huntsman, Alward, and Godus in Salisbury and Wilton; Horton manor (Glos.) from Agnes, wife of Hubert de Ria, and Henry her son; and in 1122 the four Devon churches of Kingsteignton, Harberton, Alvington, and Kenton from Serlo, royal collector in Devon.[32] Conditions attached to certain of these grants probably introduced some unwelcome influences into the chapter. The two prebends from Arnulf the Falconer had to be given in the first place to his two sons, and afterwards to clerks presented by himself or his heirs. The rich Devon prebend of Serlo was to go first to Serlo's son Richard, and afterwards to his next of kin suitable for the church; and Godalming and Heytesbury were to be held for life as a prebend by the royal servant and notorious pluralist, Ranulf Flambard, who was already Bishop of Durham.[33] Moreover, the chapter apparently did not always enjoy the rest of its property fully in Bishop Roger's lifetime. Profits from the assize of bread and ale at Stratford-sub-Castle seem to have been withdrawn by his officers before 1120, when he ordered them to be restored.[34] In 1122 he roused the canons' resentment by giving their prebend of Sherborne, with the right to a place in choir and voice in chapter, to the Abbot of Sherborne in perpetuity.[35] Finally, however, probably on his death-bed, he restored to their church all the prebends he had been keeping in his own hand, increased the tithes of their church of West Lavington, and appropriated the prebend of Bishop's Cannings to their common fund.[36]

Both before and after Bishop Roger's fall and death, Stephen, and later Maud, showed themselves very ready to confirm and extend the chapter's privileges and endowments. Stephen appropriated Odiham church, given by Henry I, with the churches or chapels of Liss and Bentworth (Hants), to the *magister scolae*, and gave 10 librates in his own domain, possibly in Salisbury, to the common fund.[37] Westbury church was appropriated to the precentor's office.[38] Heytesbury church received gifts from Maud and others which enabled Bishop Jocelin to constitute it a collegiate church with four prebends.[39] Tithes from Earl Ranulf of Chester, and, possibly, a piece of the bishop's land in south Woodford, increased the value of Wilsford prebend, held by Roger the succentor.[40] New churches and estates were also given to the chapter: Durnford church by Walter de Tony and its other patrons; Chardstock church (Dors.) by Gerbert de Percy; Bramshaw church (Hants) and Torlton manor (Glos.) by Walter of Salisbury, Sybil, his wife, and their heir, Earl Patrick of Salisbury.[41] At the same time the chapter's property clearly suffered in the wars, as is shown by successive charters of Stephen, Eugenius III, the Empress Maud, Henry II, and others, restoring to it lands and churches unjustly seized.[42] The apparent recovery of all its property, except perhaps the church and land at Wanborough, is marked by a charter of Henry II of 1158, confirming all its lands, churches, and privileges, with the additional privilege of freedom from suits of shires and hundreds.[43]

During the last 60 years of the cathedral in the

31 *Reg. St. Osmund* (Rolls Ser.), i, 200–2, 206, 208; *Sar. Chart. & Doc.* (Rolls Ser.), 3–4.

32 *Reg. St. Osmund* (Rolls Ser.), i, 202–3, 381–2; W. Farrer, *Itin. Hen. I*, no. 474.

33 *Reg. St. Osmund* (Rolls Ser.), i, 381–3, cf. 96; *Sar. Chart. & Doc.* (Rolls Ser.), 3.

34 *Sar. Chart. & Doc.* (Rolls Ser.), 5.

35 J. Fowler, *Medieval Sherborne* (Dorchester, 1951), 90–103.

36 *Reg. St. Osmund* (Rolls Ser.), i, 216–17. This charter, dated *c.* 1140–2, cannot be later than 1139, when Bishop Roger died.

37 *Reg. St. Osmund* (Rolls Ser.), i, 191–2; *Sar. Chart. & Doc.* (Rolls Ser.), 8–9.

38 *Sar. Chart. & Doc.* (Rolls Ser.), 17–18.

39 *Reg. St. Osmund* (Rolls Ser.), i, 337–52.

40 Hist. MSS. Com. *Var. Coll.* i, 369–71; *Reg. St. Osmund* (Rolls Ser.), i, 205, 265. Woodford may be Woodford (Glos.) not Woodford (Wilts.).

41 *Reg. St. Osmund* (Rolls Ser.), i, 203–5, 237, 266; Hist. MSS. Com. *Var. Coll.* i, 368; *Sar. Chart. & Doc.* (Rolls Ser.), 34–35.

42 *Sar. Chart. & Doc.* (Rolls Ser.), 9–15, 20–22, 29–30; Hist. MSS. Com. *Var. Coll.* i, 361–2; *Reg. St. Osmund* (Rolls Ser.), i, 207–8, 238, 268–9.

43 *Reg. St. Osmund* (Rolls Ser.), i, 203–6; Hist. MSS. Com. *Var. Coll.* i, 367–9. Wanborough has not been traced among the chapter's property after 1146, when Eugenius III confirmed it: *Reg. St. Osmund* (Rolls Ser.), i, 12.

royal castle of Salisbury, as the prebends gradually rose to 52 or 53, an increasing effort was made to augment the endowments of the common fund. Bishop's Cannings church was again appropriated to it by Bishop Jocelin, as were the churches of Britford, Alton Pancras (Dors.) about 1160, and probably land at East Dean (Hants) and Upway church (Dors.), given about 1201.[44] Several gifts were made specifically for it, including 'Draycott All Saints' church (unidentified), from Ralph of St. Germain about 1170, and a small piece of land at Wilton from William de Wilton, organist, about 1200.[45] About 1220 Melksham church, the gift of King John in 1200, was granted to it by Bishop Richard Poore, and on the removal to New Salisbury the prebend of Old Salisbury was dissolved and its revenues and jurisdiction divided between the bishop and the canons' common fund.[46] A further development of this period, which increased the common fund while adding to the number of prebends, followed the ending of the long dispute with Sherborne Abbey over its tenure of Sherborne prebend. As a result of awards of about 1165 and 1191, the abbey promised to pay 10 marks to the common fund within a year after the death of an abbot, and to give land at Wimborne and the churches of Lyme and Halstock (Dors.) to the chapter, in return for its recognition of the abbot as a canon and prebendary of the cathedral.[47] From this time the chapter apparently decided that such links with religious houses were both desirable and profitable. In the following years it accepted substantial gifts of property in the diocese for its common fund from three Norman abbeys in return for receiving their abbots and convents into confraternity and allowing them to hold the property of their alien priories as cathedral prebends. About 1194–1207 Upavon was constituted a prebend for the Abbot and Convent of St. Wandrille (Seine-Inférieure) in return for the churches of Whitchurch Canonicorum (Dors.) and Sherston Magna, with land and tithes at Wilsford near Manningford Bohun. About 1200–8 Ogbourne became the prebend of the Abbot and Convent of Bec (Eure) in return for the churches of Poulshot and Brixton Deverill and land at Durrington; and in 1213 Loders (Dors.) the prebend of the Abbot and Convent of St. Mary Montébourg (Manche), in return for the churches of Powerstock and Fleet (Dors.).[48] All three foreign abbots were assigned a stall in choir and a place in chapter, but were exempted from residence and agreed to maintain vicars choral to perform their duties in the cathedral. Other prebends which first appeared about this time were Bitton (Glos.) about 1200 and Chisenbury and Yatesbury about 1208–12.[49] Finally, in 1224 Honorius III granted that the common fund might be increased from revenues of Teignton prebend on condition that the number of prebends was not reduced.[50] By this time the number was 52,[51] at which figure it remained until the Reformation, thus making Salisbury one of the three largest English secular cathedral chapters. In 1226 the first known complete list of prebends and prebendaries, with some estates of the dignitaries and of the common fund, is available, with their value as assessed for papal taxation in 1217.[52] The only property in this list unaccounted for by earlier known endowments is Preston prebend (Dors.).

This assessment gives the total annual value of the chapter's property as 1,792 marks 7*s.* 4*d.*, of which the separate estates of the dignitaries and prebends accounted for 1,672 marks 7*s.* 4*d.* and those of the common fund for 120 marks. The 52 prebends varied greatly in value. Only one, Ogbourne, said to be worth £100 a year, could compare with the wealthiest York prebends of 100 to 250 marks. Two, Charminster and Teignton, the 'golden' prebends, were valued at 80 marks each, and the four poorest at less than 5 marks each. All four dignitaries had certain estates annexed to their offices, but except for the deanery, which consisted of Sonning and Mere churches,[53] these were not particularly valuable. The chantry, consisting presumably of Westbury church, was estimated at 30 marks; the chancery at 15 marks; and the treasury at 20 marks. The dean, precentor, and treasurer, who held 60-mark prebends in addition to their offices, were among the wealthiest members of the chapter, but the chancellor, with the slighter 20-mark prebend of Woodford, had a smaller income than many simple prebendaries. The assessment of the estates of the common fund at only 120 marks cannot be accepted. Only the five churches of Bishop's Cannings, Britford, Old Salisbury, Melksham, and Alton St. Pancras are mentioned. Some churches may by now have been

[44] *Reg. St. Osmund* (Rolls Ser.), i, 217–23, cf. 228, 236–7; *Sar. Chart. & Doc.* (Rolls Ser.), 64–65, 69–70, cf. 78; Leland, *Itin.* ed. Toulmin Smith, i, 265.

[45] *Reg. St. Osmund* (Rolls Ser.), i, 260–1; *Sar. Chart. & Doc.* (Rolls Ser.), 61–62.

[46] *Sar. Chart. & Doc.* (Rolls Ser.), 101–2, 167–8; *Reg. St. Osmund* (Rolls Ser.), i, 210–11, 259–60; ii, 49–50; *Rot. Chart.* (Rec. Com.), 67.

[47] *Reg. St. Osmund* (Rolls Ser.), i, 249–50; *Sar. Chart. & Doc.* (Rolls Ser.), 48–51; Hist. MSS. Com. *Var. Coll.* i, 370; cf. J. Fowler, *Medieval Sherborne*, 93–103.

[48] *Reg. St. Osmund* (Rolls Ser.), i, 229–33, 189–90, 228–9, 224–6; *Sar. Chart. & Doc.* (Rolls Ser.), 79–80.

[49] SC 12/16/57, m. 1. A fragment of rental of the chapter's manors during Interdict.

[50] *Cal. Pap. Lett.* 1198–1304, 97; *Reg. St. Osmund* (Rolls Ser.), i, 365, cf. 386–7; *Sar. Chart. & Doc.* (Rolls Ser.), 171–2.

[51] In 1229 the number was given as 53 including the bishop's prebend, perhaps because Combe and Harnham, normally united, were counted as two prebends: *Reg. St. Osmund* (Rolls Ser.), ii, 103–4; cf. *Fasti Eccl. Sar.* ed. Jones, 375.

[52] *Reg. St. Osmund* (Rolls Ser.), ii, 70–75. W. E. Lunt, *Valuation of Norw.* 526, included some churches of the common fund, omitted some prebends, and reached an incorrect total. Another valuation for 50 prebends only, probably *temp.* Ric. Poore, is in *Sar. Chart. & Doc.* (Rolls Ser.), 206–8.

[53] In 1217 the deanery, with prebend, was estimated at 133 marks 10*s.*; in 1226, perhaps in error, at only 80 marks: *Reg. St. Osmund* (Rolls Ser.), ii, 70 and n.

lost or alienated, or the chapter's share in them may have been reduced, as seems to have been the case with Henry I's gifts of King's Somborne, Alveston, and Stapleford churches, and with the more recent grants of Draycott All Saints and Upway churches.[54] The chapter's possession of the churches of Sherston Magna and Whitchurch Canonicorum was apparently still disputed.[55] But revenues from both of these as well as from Sutton Benger, Bramshaw, and Powerstock churches, the land at Durrington and Wilton, and the tithes of the royal forests were included in later assessments of the common fund,[56] and some must have been in the chapter's possession at this time. Some of these sources of income may have been deliberately suppressed in 1217 or 1226, or the copy of the assessment may be incomplete.

Some slight evidence is available to illustrate the management of this property. A few leases of separate estates or tithes have survived from the late 12th and early 13th centuries, usually to clerks, sometimes for life, for a fixed annual sum to prebendary, dignitary, or chapter.[57] Other estates, however, were under direct management. A deed of about 1179 of Bishop Jocelin approved the increase of the stock of Bedwyn prebend by 60 ewes on the chapter's advice and at the prebendary's request.[58] Of five Wiltshire estates mentioned in 1208–12 only one, Overcott (a detached portion of Shipton prebend), was then leased; the revenues of the other prebends (Chisenbury, Ratfyn, Warminster, and Yatesbury) were derived from rents of assize, corn, and stock.[59] The New Constitution of 1215 evidently reflected contemporary practice in providing either for the canon tilling the land at his own charge or letting it out to farm.[60] The form of charters and deeds suggests that the bishop's control over the chapter's property gradually loosened towards the end of the 12th century. Grants in the time of Bishop Roger and in the early years of Jocelin's episcopate were usually made in the name of the bishop and whole convent of the cathedral church;[61] later, of the bishop, dean, and chapter, or of the bishop with the dean and chapter's assent;[62] finally, about 1175, Jordan, dean, and the chapter leased a piece of land on one of the prebends in their own name, merely with the bishop's assent.[63] At the same time the chapter's assent was equally necessary, and remained so throughout the Middle Ages and later, for any alienations or leases of episcopal property. Communars or canons in charge of the common fund are first found about 1191,[64] and from about this time the individual prebendaries seem to gain more control over the administration of their prebends. By the early 13th century leases or other grants, and sometimes even vicarage ordinations on a prebend, were made in the prebendary's name and simply confirmed by bishop, dean, and chapter.[65] At the same time the dean's power to supervise affairs of the prebends was emphasized. In 1215 he was given statutory authority to visit the prebends and make corrections.[66] The only records of a decanal visitation which have survived from this period, however, are for William de Wanda's visitation of the deanery and of his own prebend of Heytesbury and Godalming between 1220 and 1226,[67] which revealed many deficiencies both in the churches and in the qualifications of some vicars and chaplains.

Meanwhile the cathedral was largely rebuilt, widened, and extended eastwards, probably about 1125–38, in the days of Bishop Roger's power.[68] It was given a square-ended choir with aisles, an ambulatory, and three chapels projecting to the east, the central one being a long, axial, square-ended Lady Chapel, which foreshadowed innovations of late 12th-century building. A crypt and cloisters were added, and a block of buildings with a large aisled hall to form the bishop's residence. William of Malmesbury says that the bishop gave many valuable ornaments to the cathedral, so that it was second to none in England,[69] though the author of the *Gesta Stephani*, who paints a less pleasing picture of Bishop Roger, says that Stephen used part of the great quantity of treasure left by the bishop for roofing the cathedral.[70] In the days of his power Bishop Roger had received from Henry I the custody of the royal castle of Salisbury,[71] and so the danger of friction between king's and bishop's men in the cramped quarters was avoided. But after the seizure of Roger's castles in 1139 no bishop of Salisbury was allowed to hold the royal castle.

Nothing like a complete list of the members of the 12th-century chapter can be compiled, but such names as have been found suggest that most elements commonly supposed to exist in 12th-century secular chapters were present at Salisbury.

54 Cf. ibid. i, 220–1, 256–9, 261–3; *Sar. Chart. & Doc.* (Rolls Ser.), 42, 100–1; *Tax. Eccl.* (Rec. Com.), 179; *Valor Eccl.* (Rec. Com.), ii, 80.

55 *Reg. St. Osmund* (Rolls Ser.), ii, 79–81; *Sar. Chart. & Doc.* (Rolls Ser.), 201–2, 261–3.

56 *Tax. Eccl.* (Rec. Com.), 182–3, 189; *Valor Eccl.* (Rec. Com.), ii, 78–81.

57 *Sar. Chart. & Doc.* (Rolls Ser.), 43–44, 59–61, 73, 78–79; *Reg. St. Osmund* (Rolls Ser.), i, 235, cf. 240, 242–3, 263–4, 266–7.

58 *Reg. St. Osmund* (Rolls Ser.), i, 252.

59 SC 12/16/57, m. 1.

60 *Stat. Sar.* 42–47.

61 *Reg. St. Osmund* (Rolls Ser.), i, 239 (the date must be in Azo's deanery, *c.* 1139–1145/8, not *c.* 1176, as given), 244–5, 266, 337, 381.

62 *Sar. Chart. & Doc.* (Rolls Ser.), 17–18, 43–44.

63 *Reg. St. Osmund* (Rolls Ser.), i, 269; cf. *Sar. Chart. & Doc.* (Rolls Ser.), 42.

64 *Sar. Chart. & Doc.* (Rolls Ser.), 52.

65 Ibid. 73; *Reg. St. Osmund* (Rolls Ser.), i, 235, 322–4.

66 *Stat. Sar.* 52–53.

67 *Reg. St. Osmund* (Rolls Ser.), i, 275–314.

68 *Arch. Jnl.* civ (1947), 140–2; A. W. Clapham, *Eng. Romanesque Archit. after the Conquest*, 45, 69, 92, 161.

69 *Gesta Regum* (Rolls Ser.), ii, 484, 547.

70 *Chrons. of Reigns of Stephen, Henry II, and Richard I* (Rolls Ser.), iii, 61.

71 *Gesta Regum* (Rolls Ser.), ii, 547.

Examples of royal clerks holding prebends have been found in all periods, with Ranulf Flambard in the early 12th century; John of Oxford, the dean forced on the chapter in defiance of its rights of election by Henry II; Master Thomas de Esseben', whom, Peter de Blois told the chapter, it would be unreasonable to compel to reside, because he was faithful, industrious, and experienced in public business of the kingdom, and necessary to the king.[72] At the same time the bishops provided for the clerks who helped them in diocesan administration and for their kinsmen. Cathedral canons and dignitaries are frequently found witnessing episcopal acts in different parts of the diocese, while a number of men who first appear in the records as bishop's clerks or chaplains later became canons.[73] Family influences were strong. Reynold FitzJocelin, Bishop Jocelin de Bohun's son, was Archdeacon of Salisbury, and another younger kinsman of the bishop, Savaric de Bohun, was treasurer.[74] Azo, the Dean, and Roger, Archdeacon of Salisbury about 1139–42, were brothers, as were Henry de Beaumont, dean, and Walter, canon, about 1163, Canons William and Jocelin de Wemberg about 1192, and the two bishops Herbert and Richard Poore at the end of the century.[75] The chapter also maintained its continental connexions, particularly with Bayeux. Henry de Beaumont became Bishop of Bayeux in 1165, and was succeeded as Dean of Salisbury by Jordan, a canon of Bayeux, who had also been Archdeacon of Salisbury. Richard de Bohun, Dean of Bayeux and later Bishop of Coutances, was a brother of Bishop Jocelin. Robert de Novo Burgo, Dean of Rouen, and William, Dean of Sens, were both canons of Salisbury (*c.* 1184–8), as was Hugh Bovet, Archdeacon of Bayeux (*c.* 1200–10).[76] A striking feature of lists of witnesses to capitular charters of the late 12th and early 13th centuries is the increasing number of *magistri*, or scholars with a licence to teach, some of whom, while studying and teaching in the growing schools or universities of Europe, must, with the royal and episcopal clerks and the pluralists, have swollen the ranks of the non-residents. Other reasons for non-residence at the cathedral doubtless lay in the rival claims on the canons of their separate prebendal estates and churches, and in the expenses of residence, with its obligation to dispense hospitality, and in the difficulty of finding a house within the royal castle. The scholar and archbishop's clerk, Peter of Blois, who held a 5-mark prebend at Salisbury towards the end of the century, indignantly told the dean and chapter that his prebend was insufficient to pay for the journey to Salisbury, and that to demand residence from all canons was unreasonable, since some were necessary to the king, some to the archbishop, some were ill, some active in the schools, and some on pilgrimage.[77]

It is impossible to discover how many canons were actually resident at this time. Lists of canons witnessing deeds at Salisbury vary usually from two or three to twelve in the pontificates of Roger, Jocelin, and Hubert Walter, rising on rare occasions to as many as 21 and 24 under Bishop Hubert Walter,[78] but these are probably not reliable guides. St. Osmund had thought it reasonable for a canon to be absent for a third of the year, but it is likely that the number of absentees exceeded his expectations almost from the start. It is not until the 12th century that we have any evidence of the methods adopted by bishop and chapter to deal with the problem. One method appears in the efforts made from about 1160 onwards to divert endowments to the common fund, which was reserved for the residentiaries, in order to make residence financially more attractive. By 1198–1200 a fine of one-fifth of the value of their prebends, also payable to the common fund, was being demanded from those who refused to reside;[79] while before 1195 the chapter had apparently already taken the bold step of reducing the minimum annual period of residence from two-thirds to a quarter of the year. These new regulations are first found in 1195 in statutes of Lichfield chapter, where they had probably been adopted from Salisbury.[80] The earliest surviving Salisbury document which gives them is the *Nova Constitutio* of 1215, which declared that a quarter of the canons must always keep residence at their statutory terms, with the four principal dignitaries, who, according to Osmund's constitution, are bound to continuous residence.[81] A rota dating probably from this time shows that in every quarter of the year a different quarter of the 52 canons was required to come into residence.[82] Most other English secular chapters

72 Above, p. 159, n. 33. *D.N.B.* s.v. Oxford; *Petri Blesensis Opera* (*Patrologia Latina*, ed Migne, 207), *Epist.* 135, c. 404.

73 Cf. e.g. *Sar. Chart. & Doc.* (Rolls Ser.), 16, 18, 19, 35, 49, 60, 64, 77; A. H. Thompson, 'Master Elias of Dereham', *Arch. Jnl.* xcviii (1941), 2–3, 7.

74 For the Bohun family tree see D. Knowles, *Episcopal Colleagues of Thomas Becket*, 18 n., 19, 159.

75 *Reg. St. Osmund* (Rolls Ser.), i, 244, 248, 351; ii, 4; *Sar. Chart. & Doc.* (Rolls Ser.), 35.

76 *Materials Hist. Becket* (Rolls Ser.), v, 212–13; vi, 106, 192; *Antiq. Cart. Eccl. Baiocensis*, ed. V. Bourrienne (Soc. Hist. de Normandie), i, nos. 156, 119, 185; *Pipe R.* 1185, 204; 1186, 167; 1187, 187; 1188, 185 (P.R.S. xxxiv, xxxvi–xxxviii); *Reg. St. Osmund* (Rolls Ser.), i, 221, 235, 241, 248, 262.

77 *Patrologia Latina*, ed. Migne, 207, *Epist.* 133, c. 395; 135, c. 404.

78 *Sar. Chart. & Doc.* (Rolls Ser.), 15–16, 18–19, 35, 43–44, 50; *Reg. St. Osmund* (Rolls Ser.), i, 215–16, 218, 245, 263–4, 381; *Stat. Sar.* 38–39; Hist. MSS. Com. *Var. Coll.* i, 348.

79 *Patrologia Latina*, ed. Migne, 207, *Epist.* 133, c. 395. This must be dated 1198–1200, because it mentions R[ic. Poore] dean, whose deanery began in 1198, and the writer died in 1200. The statute requiring the payment of fifths was first registered at Salisbury in 1215, and confirmed by Honorius III in 1219; *Stat. Sar.* 42–43; *Reg. St. Osmund* (Rolls Ser.), i, 366.

80 Wilkins, *Concilia*, i, 500; cf. *Use Sar.* i, xxxiv–xxxv, xxxvii; *Stat. Sar.* 157 n.

81 *Stat. Sar.* 42–43.

82 *Sar. Chart. & Doc.* (Rolls Ser.), 209–10; *Stat. Sar.* 156–9.

were still trying to enforce a much longer minimum period of residence of two-thirds or three-quarters of the year,[83] and the rota can hardly have been observed in practice at Salisbury, even when it was first prescribed. It would obviously sometimes be difficult and inconvenient for canons to come into residence for the precise quarter of a year required by this rota. Nevertheless it had a practical object: it avoided limiting residence to those canons who were prepared to live at Salisbury for the greater part of the year, by making it possible for others, such as scholars or canons holding prebends in other cathedrals, to come into residence for a short period each year, and so to encourage as many members of the chapter as possible to remain in touch with the cathedral.

Other constitutional developments of the 12th century, such as the chapter's increasing independence of its bishop, and the further definition of its system of home government, are conveniently summed up in the constitutional chapters of the Salisbury Consuetudinary of about 1210 and the *Nova Constitutio* of 1215.[84] These show that the dean's powers over the cathedral, its clergy, and their estates had increased at the expense of those of the bishop, which was a natural result of the growing separation of interests of bishop and chapter. During the last half of the 12th century the deans of Salisbury had generally been able men, only one of whom had failed to be promoted to a bishopric.[85] In the early 13th century the bishop still held a prebend, which entitled him to be present at chapter meetings as a prebendary,[86] if not as president, and he collated to all the other prebends except Shipton and Blewbury.[87] If he attended cathedral services he was to be treated with honour and reverence, and on certain feast days was assigned the principal part in them. He had, however, no right to celebrate out of his turn. In his frequent absences the dean took his place, and was treated with equal reverence in choir in the bishop's presence or absence.[88] The opening chapters of the Consuetudinary, which are stated to be an explanation of St. Osmund's Institution, define the dean's powers in greater detail than the Institution. It was from the dean that the canons received possession of their prebends, which he had the right to visit; he assigned their places in chapter and stalls in choir, and admitted all vicars and clerks of the second form; he heard all causes of the chapter and punished offenders; neither canons nor lesser clergy might let blood or be absent from Salisbury even for a night without his permission.[89]

The dean, however, was no more than *primus inter pares* among the canons, who, at least from about the mid-12th century, had the canonical right to elect both him and their bishop;[90] and the causes he heard were determined by judgement of the chapter,[91] which shared his growing independence of the bishop. Moreover, responsibility for administrative work at the cathedral was still divided between him and the other three great dignitaries. The Consuetudinary shows that the chancellor had established his precedence over the treasurer in the third place, which had been in doubt in the Institution.[92] He was also assigned all the functions attributed both to him and to the *archiscola* in the Institution, and had a *magister scolarum* to help him.[93] The *Nova Constitutio*, in its careful regulations for the custody and use of the chapter seals,[94] shows his increasing secretarial duties. A number of capitular deeds of the early 13th century 'given by the chancellor's hand'[95] suggest that he was doing this secretarial work in person and it is interesting to find also an isolated bishop's charter of 1222 dated at Salisbury, in which he acted as datary.[96] From about 1218 onwards, however, separate bishop's chaplains or scribes appear increasingly as dataries of the bishops' charters.[97] Unfortunately there is no evidence to show whether in earlier times the cathedral chancellor had normally acted as secretary to both bishop and chapter.[98] Further details are also given in the Consuetudinary of the treasurer's obligations to furnish lights in the cathedral, to direct and maintain the sacrists and the bell-ringing, to repair the church's ornaments, and to provide bread and wine for the altars.[99] The chanter is now said to be responsible for the instruction and discipline of the boy choristers, whose duties are described.[1] Some of the most illuminating work of definition in early 13th-century documents concerns the vicars choral.

[83] Edwards, *Eng. Secular Cath.* 51–56.

[84] *Use Sar.* i, 1 sqq.; *Stat. Sar.* 40–53.

[85] Robert became Bp. of Exeter, 1155; Henry de Beaumont Bp. of Bayeux, 1165; John of Oxford Bp. of Norw. 1175; Jordan apparently died as dean; Eustace became Bp. of Ely 1197; Richard Poore successively Bp. of Chich., Sar. and Dur.

[86] *Sar. Chart. & Doc.* (Rolls Ser.), 95. In 1219 the prebend of *Major Pars Altaris* was exchanged for Horton, and in 1254 Horton for Potterne, which the bp. still holds: *Reg. St. Osmund* (Rolls Ser.), i, 196–7.

[87] Cf. *Sar. Chart. & Doc.* (Rolls Ser.), 102–5, 173–4, 123–4, 126; *Reg. St. Osmund* (Rolls Ser.), i, 327–8.

[88] *Use Sar.* i, from Index, s.v. *decanus*.

[89] *Use Sar.* 2, 8; *Stat. Sar.* 52–53.

[90] Bp. Roger was apparently elected by clergy and people; Bp. Jocelin in 1142 by the chapter; cf. *E.H.R.* (1952), 565; D. Knowles, *Episcopal Colleagues of Becket*, 7. The first evidence of the chapter's right to elect its dean is in 1165, when Hen. II informed Bp. Jocelin of his wish that John of Oxford, his clerk, should be appointed and a papal prohibition safeguarded the rights in the election of those of the chapter who were in exile with Archbp. Becket: *Materials Hist. Becket* (Rolls Ser.), v, 416, 375.

[91] *Use Sar.* i, 2, 8–10.

[92] Ibid. i, 3–4.

[93] Ibid. i, 3–4, 104.

[94] *Stat. Sar.* 40–43.

[95] *Reg. St. Osmund* (Rolls Ser.), i, 323, 325, 379; ii, 33; *Sar. Chart. & Doc.* (Rolls Ser.), 79, 86, 233; *Cat. Anct. D.* iii, D 382 (p. 449).

[96] *Sar. Chart. & Doc.* (Rolls Ser.), i, 121.

[97] Ibid. 84, 99, 122, 189, 199, 229, 237–8; *Reg. St. Osmund* (Rolls Ser.), i, 322; ii, 25, 29.

[98] Cf. C. R. Cheney, *Eng. Bps.' Chanceries*, 39.

[99] *Use Sar.* i, 4–7.

[1] Ibid. 3, and index, s.v. *Puer*.

Constitutions of 1214 and 1222 make it clear that every canon, resident or non-resident, was bound to have a vicar to sing and acquit him in the cathedral services;[2] and a list of names of 52 vicars choral at Salisbury survives from 1297.[3] From the first they were apparently supposed to be in the order of priest, deacon, or sub-deacon required by their master's prebend,[4] and were nominated by their masters. But they were admitted by the dean only after examination, and were on probation for a year until they knew the psalter and antiphoner by heart.[5] Their important charter or constitution of 1214 laid down that they could be removed only for some grave fault. It also granted them the right to accept legacies and other gifts of property in common, in addition to their fixed annual payment or stall wages from their masters' prebends and 1*d.* a day each for commons from the chapter.[6]

These statutes 'On the Condition of the Vicars', issued by Richard Poore and his chapter, seem to have given a lead to other cathedral chapters similar to that given earlier by St. Osmund's constitution.[7] The innovations of the early 13th-century chapter, however, must not be exaggerated, for much of the work was probably based on 12th-century precedents, now lost. The grant of security of tenure to the vicars choral was not a new act of legislation in 1214, for they apparently already had it in about 1185–9 and in 1194, when vicars of the deceased bishop and canons were paid their stipends from the revenues of the vacant prebends by the keepers of the bishopric.[8]

NEW SALISBURY

The first half or three-quarters of the 13th century seems to have been the time when the prestige, influence, prosperity, independence, and corporate spirit of the chapter reached their peak. The chapter formed a remarkably distinguished body of men, including a number of able scholars and statesmen, some of European fame: Master Richard Poore, dean and later bishop; St. Edmund of Abingdon, treasurer, the saintly scholar who became Archbishop of Canterbury; his successor as treasurer, Master John of St. Albans, a pupil of Stephen Langton at Paris; Master Henry of Bishopstone, a doctor of canon law of Oxford, who ruled the school in the new city of Salisbury; Master Roger of Salisbury, who lectured in theology there; Master Robert Bingham, Richard Poore's successor as Bishop of Salisbury; Master Elias of Dereham, '*incomparabilis artifex*', who supervised the building of the new cathedral; Master Thomas de Chabham, sub-dean, author of the *Summa de Penitentia*; William de Wanda, the chapter's historian.[9] For the first time records survive of large general chapters attended by about 17 to 39 canons, held under the presidency of Richard Poore as dean and bishop to approve his large schemes for the codification of the cathedral customs and liturgy, for the building of a new cathedral, and for the canonization of St. Osmund. At such chapters the *Nova Constitutio*, and, probably, the Salisbury Consuetudinary and Ordinal were published.[10] In these documents the 'four-square' constitution is found in all essentials, and the Use of Salisbury which was soon to influence other dioceses was launched. The active and statesmanlike part taken by the canons at such meetings may be illustrated from their recorded discussions at a chapter of 1226,[11] which met to debate Henry III's demand for a tax on the spiritualities of the clergy and which shows Salisbury giving leadership to the English Church. Its suggestion that proctors from all English cathedral churches should be summoned to deliberate on the grant was adopted by Archbishop Langton, and had important results on the history of Convocation.[12] Moreover, the meeting of proctors which followed unanimously accepted the proposals which Salisbury chapter had instructed its representatives to make.[13]

The most outstanding example of the initiative of bishop, dean, and chapter at this time, however, was their decision to abandon their cathedral in the royal castle of Salisbury, and to build a new one below in the Avon valley. Their reasons are set out in the chapter's account of the inconveniences of their site sent to the Pope in 1217. They were dominated and oppressed by the castellan and soldiers in the castle; they were not allowed to go in and out without leave from the castellan; the faithful were not allowed to visit the church; many cathedral clerks were deterred from residence by lack of dwellings; the continuous gusts of wind round the hill made such a noise that they could hardly hear one another sing; the place was liable to give them colds in the head (*reomaticus*); the church was shaken by wind and storm; the site was without trees and grass and the glare from the chalk had blinded many clerks; water was only to be got at a distance and at a high price.[14] Obviously such disadvantages had not just become apparent. Probably friction between the royal garrison and cathedral establishment did not become acute until Stephen's seizure of Bishop Roger's castles in 1139. In the time of

[2] *Stat. Sar.* 48–51, 74–77.
[3] *Cal. Pat.* 1292–1301, 266.
[4] Cf. *Stat. Sar.* 214–17.
[5] Ibid. 74–77.
[6] Ibid. 48–51.
[7] *Use Sar.* i, xxvii, xxxvi–xxxvii.
[8] *Pipe R.* 1186, 167; 1187, 87; 1188, 185; 1194, 256 (P.R.S. xxxvi–xxxviii, N.S. v).
[9] Cf. M. Gibbs and J. Lang, *Bps. and Reform 1215–72*, from Index; *Reg. St. Osmund* (Rolls Ser.), ii, 3; D. Callus in *Oxoniensia*, x, 50–53; *Arch. Jnl.* xcviii (1941), 1–35.
[10] *Stat. Sar.* 52–53, 70–71; *Reg. St. Osmund* (Rolls Ser.), ii, 7–8, 10–11, 14–19, 33–34, 37, 41–43, 55–70. The Consuetudinary and Ordinal were probably both published *c.* 1210; *Use Sar.* i, xix–xx; ii, vii.
[11] *Reg. St. Osmund* (Rolls Ser.), ii, 55–70.
[12] D. B. Weske, *Convocation of the Clergy*, 43–44, 200–3; M. V. Clarke, *Medieval Representation and Consent*, 265–7.
[13] *Reg. St. Osmund* (Rolls Ser.), ii, 64–70.
[14] Reg. Vat. ix, ff. 90*b*–91; Reg. St. Osmund (Sar. Dioc. Regy.), f. 60*b*; *Cal. Pap. Lett.* 1198–1304, 46, 53, translates *reomaticus* as rheumatic; *Reg. St. Osmund* (Rolls Ser.), ii, 5–6, gives *ruinatus* in error for *reumaticus*.

Bishop Herbert Poore the canons frequently discussed moving their cathedral to a freer and more commodious site. Probably about 1198–9, after Richard Poore's appointment as dean and before King Richard's death, the decision was made. The bishop obtained permission from the king; a site was chosen, and a plot of land on which to build a house assigned to each canon.[15] Canon Peter of Blois wrote before 1200 apologizing for not coming to the distribution of the houses, saying, 'Let us descend joyfully to the plains, where the valley abounds in corn, where the fields are beautiful, and where there is freedom from oppression.'[16] His words are echoed in a poem of Henry of Avranches, who described the building of the new cathedral. The old site had been as the mountains of Gilboa, without rain, dew, flowers, or grass, where no nightingale sings: where there is only the castle and the wind. Of the new site, he wrote that Adam would have preferred it to Paradise.[17]

Probably the site was that of the present cathedral by the river in a meadow belonging to the bishop's group of manors which in the 12th century were known as Old Salisbury.[18] The traditional story of Bishop Richard Poore being led some 20 years later by a dream to choose this meadow called 'Myrifeld' is obviously confused and legendary.[19] However, nothing more was accomplished in Bishop Herbert's pontificate. William de Wanda, canon and later dean, who wrote the vivid contemporary chronicle of the cathedral's translation, blamed Herbert personally for the failure, but, as William acknowledged, the bishop suffered great losses during the Interdict.[20] About the time of his death in February 1217 the dean and chapter again took up the plan, petitioning the Pope for permission to move their cathedral.[21] A few months later, the appointment as bishop of Herbert's brother, Richard Poore, brought a new spirit of energy, determination, unselfishness, and spiritual power into the work. The new bishop sent his messengers to Rome to help those of the chapter, and summoned a general convocation of all the canons to discuss the move. In 1219, soon after the papal bull authorizing the removal was received, a churchyard was consecrated and a wooden chapel built.[22] The bishop had already provided himself with a residence called New Place at Old Salisbury by the river.[23] On 28 April 1220 the foundation stones of the new cathedral were laid.[24] Very soon the practice developed of referring to the new cathedral and the new bishop's city growing up round it as New Salisbury; to the royal borough on the mound as Old Salisbury.[25]

The building of the new Gothic cathedral took nearly a century, though the essential parts were completed in the first 30 years. By 1225 the east end had progressed far enough for three altars to be consecrated at an impressive ceremony at which Archbishop Stephen Langton preached to the people; and Henry III and many magnates visited it shortly afterwards.[26] The consecration of the whole church was in 1258. It was roofed with lead and completed by 1266, with a great belfry west of the cathedral. The chapter house and cloisters were begun between 1263 and 1271 and took about ten years to build; at the end of the 13th and beginning of the 14th centuries the tower was heightened and the spire added.[27] The whole is remarkable for its uniformity of design and the beauty of its external outline. At the same time the canons were planning one of the most beautiful cathedral closes in the world. The cathedral was to stand in the midst of a wide open space with the exceptionally large and lovely cloisters on its south; on the east walk, as in a monastery, was the entry to the chapter house; the bishop's palace lay to the south, and the houses of the canons and vicars choral were ranged upon the edges of the close, some, along the west walk, with gardens nearly a tenth of a mile in length, leading down to the river which formed the western boundary.[28] The effective enclosure with a crenellated stone wall on the remaining three sides, and three stone gateways, was only completed with stones from their former cathedral and houses at Old Salisbury in the 1330's,[29] but the building of the houses began in 1219. A meeting of bishop, dean, and chapter on 15 August 1219 decided that the move should be made on 1 November by those canons who wished to move and could. Both canons and vicars had to bear the expense of building their own houses, and at a further chapter meeting in August 1222 it was decreed that everyone who had a site must begin to build by next Whitsun, or the bishop would dispose of the site. In partial recompense for their initial outlay, the houses of the first builders might be sold after their death by their heirs or assigns for two-thirds of the just price, the remaining third going to the cathedral fabric fund; but only cathedral clergy might buy the houses, and the builder's successor in his canonry or vicarage was to be given preference in the purchase.[30] One of the first houses was the large stone house called Leadenhall in the West Walk built at great expense by Master Elias of Dereham as a pattern

[15] *Reg. St. Osmund* (Rolls Ser.), ii, 3.
[16] *Patrologia Latina*, ed. Migne, 207, *Epist.* 104.
[17] *W.A.M.* xxx, 211, 216.
[18] This will be discussed under the history of Old Salisbury.
[19] *Sar. Chart. & Doc.* (Rolls Ser.), 266–9.
[20] *Reg. St. Osmund*, ii, 3–4.
[21] *Cal. Pap. Lett.* 1198–1304, 46.
[22] *Reg. St. Osmund* (Rolls Ser.), ii, 4, 5, 7, 10.
[23] *Sar. Chart. & Doc.* (Rolls Ser.), 84.
[24] *Reg. St. Osmund* (Rolls Ser.), ii, 12.
[25] *Rot. Litt. Claus.* (Rec. Com.), i, 466.
[26] *Reg. St. Osmund* (Rolls Ser.), ii, 38–40, 43–44.
[27] *Arch. Jnl.* civ (1947), 144.
[28] *Brit. Arch. Jnl.* 3rd ser. iv (1939), 61–62.
[29] *Cal. Pat.* 1327–30, 159; 1330–4, 234; W. Dodsworth, *Hist. Account Sar.* (1814), 146–7.
[30] *Reg. St. Osmund* (Rolls Ser.), ii, 10, 21.

for a canon's residence.[31] The resident architect seems to have been a mason, Master Nicholas of Ely, who was provided with a messuage in the new city for himself and his heirs about 1230.[32] It is, however, clear that the burden of organization fell mainly on the dean and chapter, and particularly on their appointed deputy, Master Elias of Dereham, who held the offices of keeper of the fabric and common funds from at least 1224–5.[33] Henry III made many gifts of timber and money,[34] and in 1225, when the dean and chapter committed the offerings at the newly consecrated high altar to the bishop for seven years, the bishop at once gave them into the keeping of Elias, 'having at that time no confidence in the trustworthiness of any other person'.[35] Not all the cathedral clergy were willing to make the sacrifices in time and money demanded from them by bishop and chapter. At the beginning in 1219 it was agreed that all canons, resident and non-resident, with the vicars and chaplains should contribute a fixed portion to the fabric from their prebends and stipends for seven years. Then the bishop suggested that the vicars choral should be sent to preach and collect alms throughout the country. Some at first agreed to go, but the next day all refused, and so seven dignitaries and canons took their places, and were absent for a long time, travelling in some cases as far as Scotland and Ireland.[36] In 1222 another general chapter meeting attended by the bishop and 30 canons attempted to meet the grievances of those canons who felt themselves over-burdened by expense, by reducing the minimum annual residence for the following 3 years to 40 days for the canons and 21 days for the archdeacons (except the Archdeacon of Salisbury).[37] In 1225 it was found necessary to extend these concessions and the grant of a subsidy from the prebends for a further seven years.[38] The non-residents then objected that they should therefore no longer be bound to pay the fifth part of the income of their prebends to the use of the residentiaries, and it was finally agreed that, for the next seven years, they should pay a tenth instead.[39] Yet, in spite of all the difficulties and the reluctance of some, money was found; indulgences were granted to those who contributed; magnificent offerings were made by Henry III, who took a very special interest in the work, as well as by Hubert de Burgh and the magnates; and there were many lesser gifts from humbler folk.[40] A severe blow came in 1228 when Bishop Richard Poore was translated to Durham, but the work went on under later bishops and deans trained in his service or as his colleagues in the chapter. Only one of his plans was not followed: that of obtaining the canonization of Bishop Osmund, the chapter's founder. One of Poore's last acts as Bishop of Salisbury was to write to the dean and chapter urging them to press on with this business, but after his translation to Durham the matter was allowed to drop.[41] Undoubtedly the plan would have required a heavy outlay, but it was far-sighted, and, had it been carried through, the offerings at the saint's shrine might have amply repaid it.

The 13th-century chapter became an increasingly powerful, independent, and wealthy body. This is seen particularly in the way it was able to elect a surprisingly large number of its bishops and deans *de gremio*. The period following King John's grant of freedom to the English Church and the legislation of the Fourth Lateran Council of 1215 was the time when free elections were given a trial in England. Cathedral reform in accordance with the Lateran decrees, as it was carried through under Richard Poore, seems to have given the chapter independence and capacity to withstand external influences of king, pope, and magnates. From 1228 until 1284 four out of five bishops were successively elected *de gremio*,[42] with only a short interval from 1246–56 when the see was held by a royal clerk, William of York. In the same period the chapter's prestige is shown by the choice of others of its members to be bishops of other dioceses: Master Roger of Salisbury, the precentor, went to Bath and Wells; St. Edmund of Abingdon, the treasurer, to Canterbury, and Henry of Lexington, a later treasurer, to Lincoln. Moreover, elections *de gremio* continued, though more intermittently, into the late 13th and early 14th centuries. In 1284 and 1287 two more deans of Salisbury were elected as bishops in quick succession, though both these, Master Walter Scammell and Master Henry de Brandeston, had also acted as royal clerks and their appointments were probably pleasing to the king. The choice of William de la Corner and of Nicholas Longespée, treasurer of Salisbury, a son of William Longespée, Earl of Salisbury, may have been due to royal or baronial influence respectively, but the elections of 1297 and 1315 resulted in the appointment

31 *Sar. Chart. & Doc.* (Rolls Ser.), 203–5; *W.A.M.* xxxix, 441.

32 Hist. MSS. Com. *Var. Coll.* i, 382.

33 *Arch. Jnl.* xcviii (1941), 1–35.

34 e.g. *Rot. Litt. Claus.* (Rec. Com.), i, 539; ii, 91*b*; *Close R.* 1231–4, 370; 1234–7, 279–80, 409; *Cal. Lib. R.* 1240–5, 222.

35 *Reg. St. Osmund* (Rolls Ser.), ii, 44.

36 Ibid. ii, 8–9, 11–12; *Pat. R.* 1216–25, 339.

37 *Reg. St. Osmund* (Rolls Ser.), ii, 18–19; *Stat. Sar.* 70–73.

38 *Reg. St. Osmund* (Rolls Ser.), ii, 41. The subsidy was again extended for 7 years in 1233: *Sar. Chart. & Doc.* (Rolls Ser.), 229–30.

39 *Reg. St. Osmund* (Rolls Ser.), ii, 41.

40 Hist. MSS. Com. *Var. Coll.* i, 369–70, 375, 377–9; *Sar. Chart. & Doc.* (Rolls Ser.), 236–8, 329, 343–4; *Reg. St. Osmund* (Rolls Ser.), ii, 10, 13, 38–39, 43–44, 48; *Cal. Chart. R.* 1226–57, 218; *Pat. R.* 1216–25, 257; *Rot. Litt. Claus.* (Rec. Com.), *passim*; *Close R.* 1231–61, *passim*; *Cal. Lib. R.* 1226–51, *passim*.

41 *Reg. St. Osmund* (Rolls Ser.), ii, 87–89; cf. *Canonization of St. Osmund*, ed. A. R. Malden (Wilts. Rec. Soc.), iii.

42 *Reg. St. Osmund* (Rolls Ser.), ii, 102–16; *Cal. Pat.* 1247–58, 492; *Sar. Chart. & Doc.* (Rolls Ser.), 336–40, 351–4.

of two of Salisbury's most distinguished scholar bishops, Master Simon of Ghent and Master Roger Mortival. At the same time the 13th-century deans, except perhaps Master Henry de Brandeston from 1285–7, seem normally to have been freely elected in large chapters of both resident and non-resident canons, and to have been conscientious and learned men, usually resident at the cathedral.[43] This continued until the appointment about 1297 of Peter of Savoy, the first of the non-resident foreign deans.

The ability of the chapter to increase its independence of its bishops without any noticeable conflict with them may have been partly due to the fact that many of its bishops had had experience as canons or deans of the chapter's traditions. The most remarkable event was in 1262 when Bishop Giles of Bridport declared that, from his examination of Blessed Osmund's constitution and the Salisbury customs, he had decided that none of his predecessors had exercised or demanded a visitation. He granted that all members of the cathedral church and of the canons' prebends should for the future be exempt from episcopal visitation; that visitation of the cathedral and prebends belonged only to the dean, as did the admission and institution of vicars to the prebendal churches. Correction of vicars both on the prebends and at the cathedral church was to be made only by the dean and chapter, and the only power and jurisdiction reserved to the bishop was the presentation to him of vicars of the prebendal churches on his own manors.[44] This was a surprising surrender of episcopal claims at a time when popes were urging bishops to assert their rights to visit their cathedral chapters.[45] The result was that Salisbury chapter remained exempt from episcopal visitation until nearly the end of the 14th century, although it apparently had to submit to metropolitical visitations, at least from the time of Archbishop Pecham.[46] At the same time the co-operation of the chapter with its bishops is shown both by the way in which many of its members helped the bishop in diocesan work, and in the steps it took to protect episcopal jurisdiction and property during vacancies of the see. These steps are also striking illustrations of the chapter's powers. When the archbishops of Canterbury in the 13th century asserted their exclusive claims to exercise episcopal jurisdiction in the spiritualities of vacant sees of the province, Salisbury was one of the first cathedral chapters to oppose them, and, in 1262, to negotiate a composition with Archbishop Boniface which in practice saved much of the authority for the chapter or its members.[47] The bulk of the power went to an official chosen by the archbishop from a list of three or four canons submitted by the chapter. The official had to pay one-third of the profits of the see to the dean and chapter, who retained complete control of their own affairs, and also gained the right to exercise the episcopal jurisdiction, *sede vacante*, over certain religious houses of the diocese. In the vacancy of 1271 they paid a fine of 3,000 marks to the king for the custody of the temporalities, including knights' fees and advowsons.[48] In 1317 such temporary arrangements were converted into a permanent agreement by which the chapter assumed responsibility for the custody of the bishop's temporalities (excluding knights' fees and advowsons, which the king refused to surrender) in all future vacancies at a rent of £1,016 a year.[49]

At the same time the chapter's own property was increasing. The *Taxation of Pope Nicholas* of 1291 gives its total annual value as £2,013 13*s*. 4*d*. or 3,020 marks 6*s*. 8*d*.[50] as compared with 1,792 marks 7*s*. 4*d*. in 1217. Methods of assessment were undoubtedly stricter in 1291, and an increase in the productive value of the property may also partially account for the higher total.[51] In the case of the common fund the assessment is more complete than that of 1226 (it is valued at £329 6*s*. 8*d*. or 493 marks 16*s*. 8*d*. as against 120 marks in 1226), though several smaller pieces of property, particularly temporalities, are omitted, and no notice is taken of endowments given for the vicars choral, for chantries or obits, or the cathedral fabric. A further main difficulty is that all property outside the diocese, whether belonging to the prebends, dignities, or common fund, is excluded. Thus it is extremely difficult to obtain from it a general view of the changes which had taken place. However, it seems that the flow of endowments to the cathedral continued at a fairly even rate throughout the last three-quarters of the 13th century. The rate was slower than in the 12th and early 13th centuries, but the period was still profitable in smaller gifts.

In the dignities and prebends there were few changes apart from vicarage ordinations, which increased greatly in number in the period following the Fourth Lateran Council, compositions about tithes and chapels, and a few small additions or exchanges of lands or rents. It was by now the chapter's settled policy that additional endowments should, whenever possible, be appropriated to the common fund of the residentiaries, but as this fund gradually increased it was decided to lighten certain burdens of the individual dignitaries and prebendaries. Two of the richer prebends, Calne and Brixworth, were appropriated about 1226 and 1240 to the treasurer and chancellor, whose

[43] *Reg. St. Osmund* (Rolls Ser.), ii, 15–17; *Sar. Chart. & Doc.* (Rolls Ser.), 352–3; Hist. MSS. Com. *Var. Coll.* i, 355. Lists of witnesses suggest that 13th-cent. deans were normally resident: *Sar. Chart. & Doc.* (Rolls Ser.), *passim*.

[44] *Stat. Sar.* 96–99.

[45] Cf. Edwards, *Eng. Secular Cath.* 129–34.

[46] I. J. Churchill, *Canterbury Administration*, i, 297; ii, 143–4.

[47] Ibid. i, 161; ii, 55–59; *Stat. Sar.* 100–11.

[48] *Cal. Pat.* 1266–72, 543–4.

[49] *Cal. Fine R.* 1307–19, 348–9, cf. 236, 347; *Cal. Chanc. Wts.* i, 470; *Cal. Chart. R.* 1327–41, 122–3.

[50] *Tax. Eccl.* (Rec. Com.), 183.

[51] Cf. Lunt, *Valuation of Norw.* 17–18, 106–29, 525–6.

expenses had noticeably increased as a result of the move to New Salisbury.[52] This gave them not only greater wealth but also the certainty of a voice in the chapter. In 1222 it was decided that the estates of all four dignitaries, whose expenses for hospitality were particularly heavy, should in future receive, for a full year after death, half the fruits of their dignities and all the fruits of any prebends they held. Moreover, as soon as the common fund had increased by another 100 marks a year, a deceased prebendary's estate also was to receive the fruits of his prebend for a full year after death; in the following year his successor was to have them, and the common fund was to receive nothing.[53]

All the gifts of property to the common fund were apparently in the diocese. Among the churches acquired were St. Martin's, Salisbury, with Stratford-sub-Castle chapel;[54] Warminster, given by William Mauduit, later Earl of Warwick, in 1259;[55] Idmiston;[56] Littleton Drew, given by Walter Drew of Littleton in 1274;[57] Homington, and Chitterne St. Mary.[58] In addition, a messuage and land at Quidhampton was given by Walter Noswych, Maud, his wife, and Roger, his son, in 1273, and small pieces of property at 'Le Hurst' in West Lavington, Fisherton Anger, Salisbury, and Knighton in Figheldean were added to other lay fees of the chapter to form a fund known as 'Our Lady's Chamber' for distribution to the poor.[59] In Dorset, Fleet church was exchanged for that of Stourpaine at Bishop Bingham's request in 1245,[60] and Hilton church was probably acquired about the same time.[61] In Berkshire an annual pension of £10 was paid by Reading Abbey from 1239,[62] but the only other endowment received there, a moiety of the fruits of Chilton church given by Bishop Poore in 1233, does not seem to have been retained.[63] Few permanent endowments were given to the cathedral fabric at this time, but a beginning was made with Henry III's grant of all amercements of tenants on the lands of bishop or chapter which could belong to royal officers (except those arising from pleas of the Crown), and a few small rents mostly in and near Salisbury.[64] This period also witnessed the beginning of separate provisions for the lesser cathedral clergy. The vicars' choral most munificent benefactor was Bishop Richard Poore, whose objects were to augment their stipends and increase the services and worship in his new cathedral. In 1225 he instituted a daily sung Mass of the Blessed Virgin Mary, and gave to the vicars, who were to act as clerks for the mass, 40 marks a year for lights.[65] Shortly afterwards, in place of this he gave Bremhill church with Highway chapel and land at Stratford-sub-Castle to provide 1*d.* a day payable by the succentor to each of thirteen vicars present at the mass.[66] He is also thought to have appropriated Laverstock church to them for the same purpose.[67] In 1264 Master Robert Kareville, the cathedral treasurer, left them 100 marks in his will to purchase a rent from which each vicar might receive 1*d.* a day for ever, in the hope that they would attend divine service more willingly and devoutly and remember him in their prayers.[68] A pension of £20 a year payable by Hyde Abbey was probably received about the end of the century,[69] and in 1297 some lay fees or portions devised in aid of their food with small houses for their residence were taken into the king's hands for non-payment of the tenth demanded from the clergy.[70] A common seal of the vicars choral is thought to date from the 13th century,[71] and they probably administered their property themselves.

At the same time chantry masses and obits were providing further additions to the vicars' stipends and the residentiaries' common fund, while increasing the cathedral's services and adding to its clergy. Few have been traced at Old Salisbury,[72] though in 1219 it was arranged that chaplains as well as canons and vicars should contribute to the cost of building the new cathedral; and by 1222 two priests at least were being appointed annually and paid 50*s.* a year each to celebrate daily masses for the souls of departed bishops.[73] Between about 1219 and 1300 the foundation of eight chantries

52 *Reg. St. Osmund* (Rolls Ser.), ii, 25–26; *Sar. Chart. & Doc.* (Rolls Ser.), 259–60.

53 *Stat. Sar.* 72–75.

54 *Tax. Eccl.* (Rec. Com.), 182; cf. *Sar. Chart. & Doc.* (Rolls Ser.), 91; and below, p. 386.

55 *Sar. Chart. & Doc.* (Rolls Ser.), 329–32.

56 Idmiston church is first named as belonging to the common fund in 1282: *Reg. St. Osmund* (Rolls Ser.), ii, 34. It was omitted from the 1291 assessment, but appears in *Valor Eccl.* (Rec. Com.), ii, 78.

57 *Feet of F.* 1272–1327 (W.A.S. Rec. Brch.), 3.

58 These two churches are first found among benefices of the common fund in *Tax. Eccl.* (Rec. Com.), 182.

59 *Feet of F.* 1272–1327 (W.A.S. Rec. Brch.), 2, 14; *Cal. Close R.* 1296–1302, 20.

60 *Sar. Chart. & Doc.* (Rolls Ser.), 292–3.

61 Hilton church, possibly given by Bp. Bingham, whose obit was charged on it, is first found belonging to the dean and chapter in *Tax. Eccl.* (Rec. Com.), 182; cf. *Valor Eccl.* (Rec. Com.), ii, 78.

62 Hist. MSS. Com. *Var. Coll.* i, 373; cf. *Valor Eccl.* (Rec. Com.), ii, 81.

63 *Sar. Chart. & Doc.* (Rolls Ser.), 228–9, cf. 125.

64 Ibid. 180–2, 236–8, 365; Hist. MSS. Com. *Var. Coll.* i, 369–70, 375; *Cal. Chart. R.* 1226–57, 218; *Close R.* 1242–7, 492; *Cal. Inq. p.m.* ii, 271, 307; *Cat. Anct. D.* iii, D. 291 (pp. 438–9).

65 *Reg. St. Osmund* (Rolls Ser.), ii, 38–39.

66 *Sar. Chart. & Doc.* (Rolls Ser.), 116–19.

67 *Fasti Eccl. Sar.* ed. Jones, 271; *Valor Eccl.* (Rec. Com.), ii, 84.

68 *Sar. Chart. & Doc.* (Rolls Ser.), 345.

69 The annual payment of £20 by Hyde Abbey to the vicars is recorded in 1535, with pensions of 13*s.* 4*d.* and 6*s.* 8*d.* to the dean and chapter from Collingbourne and Pewsey churches: *Valor Eccl.* (Rec. Com.), ii, 80, 84. These probably originated in the late 13th cent. when the abbey had permission to alienate the churches to the dean and chapter in order to pay the £20, but apparently it preferred to continue paying the pensions instead: *Cal. Pat.* 1281–92, 230, 495.

70 *Cal. Close R.* 1296–1302, 18.

71 See below, p. 210.

72 *Reg. St. Osmund* (Rolls Ser.), i, 210–12, 219–20, 228; cf. *Valor Eccl.* (Rec. Com.), ii, 78.

73 *Stat. Sar.* 76–77; *Reg. St. Osmund* (Rolls Ser.), ii, 11, 22.

Seth Ward, Bishop of Salisbury, 1667–1689

John Wordsworth, Bishop of Salisbury, 1885–1911

or daily masses[74] and at least nineteen obits[75] has been traced, and a messuage in Malmesbury was given by Roger de Brinkworth for a taper to burn on feast days before the altar of relics for his soul.[76] The founders of daily masses and obits were mostly bishops, deans, and other cathedral clergy, including a vicar choral, John de Hospitali; only one, Edmund, Earl of Cornwall, was an important lay magnate. Two hundred or 220 marks was sufficient to found a daily mass, and 100 marks or less to found an annual obit service.[77] In a few cases these amounts were given to local religious houses on condition that they paid from 5 to 10 marks a year to the cathedral communar to provide for the obit or chantry.[78] More often, property was given direct to the dean and chapter's common fund.[79] A favourite device of canons wishing to found an obit was to leave their canonical houses in the close to the dean and chapter, on condition that they assigned them to future residentiary canons who were to pay a small obit rent for the annual services.[80] Probably few additional cathedral clergy were provided by the chantries. No chantry was yet served by more than one chaplain, and in several cases vicars choral already at the cathedral were appointed to them.[81] The foundation deed of Sir John Dacy's chantry, however, expressly laid down that the chaplain was not to be a vicar choral.[82]

Finally, in the 13th century the chapter's prestige was enhanced by the way in which the new cathedral and city became a centre of learning and art. Probably this was largely due to the stimulus of Richard Poore and the learned group of canons whom he gathered round him, as well as to the demands of the new fabric and the influence of the skilled craftsmen who were brought from a distance to work on it. No evidence has been found that the cathedral school at Old Salisbury developed teaching in the higher faculties of law and theology or attracted students from a distance like contemporary cathedral schools elsewhere in the later 12th century.[83] This development seems at Salisbury to have taken place in the 13th century, when the existence of two English universities at Oxford and Cambridge was drawing the better students away from other cathedral schools. A cathedral school was established very early at New Salisbury, as soon as the building of the cathedral was begun. In 1220 Master Henry of Bishopstone, canon of Salisbury, who had previously lectured in canon law at Oxford, was ruling the school in the new city, while in 1225, when Henry had ceased to reside, Master Roger of Salisbury, the precentor, was lecturing in theology there.[84] By 1240 the duty of providing and paying a theologian or of giving theology lectures himself, in addition to providing a grammar-school master, definitely belonged to the chancellor. Brixworth prebend was then permanently annexed to the chancellor's office at the request of the chancellor Adam de Esseby, who already held it, to enable his successors to support their increased educational burdens.[85] About this time the cathedral schools and the chancellor's reponsibilities for their scholars were expanding in a remarkable way. In 1238 there was a migration of masters and students from Oxford to Salisbury and Northampton,[86] and some apparently continued at Salisbury and may have been reinforced by the troubles of 1264 or by one of the many disturbances of 1264–8 at Oxford.[87] An award of 1279 between the chancellor and sub-dean, who both claimed jurisdiction over the scholars, shows that most of the essentials of a *studium generale* or university then existed at Salisbury.[88] It was doubtless for students in this nascent university that Bishop Giles of Bridport founded his House of Valley Scholars in 1262[89] and Bishop Walter de la Wyle his collegiate church of St. Edmund.[90] At the same time there is evidence for the intellectual interests of some residentiary canons, particularly the chancellors Master Simon de Micham, Master Ralph of York, Master William de Bosco, and Master Henry de la Wyle. Some scholastic manuscripts, histories, and theological and philosophical works, still in the cathedral library, were originally owned and given to the library by them, and a few of their theological *quaestiones* disputed at Oxford are extant.[91] Certain cathedral clergy seem to have encouraged the production of illuminated manuscripts of high artistic quality at Salisbury.[92]

74 *Sar. Chart. & Doc.* (Rolls Ser.), 215–17, 325–8, 342–3, 349–50; *Reg. St. Osmund* (Rolls Ser.), i, 390–3; Hist. MSS. Com. *Var. Coll.* i, 375; *Valor Eccl.* (Rec. Com.), ii, 79, 87.

75 *Sar. Chart. & Doc.* (Rolls Ser.), 101–2, 203–5, 215–17, 325–6, 331–4, 341–3; *Reg. St. Osmund* (Rolls Ser.), i, 390–3; Hist. MSS. Com. *Var. Coll.* i, 345, 370; E 36/57, f. 12*b*; *Valor Eccl.* (Rec. Com.), ii, 78–79, 81–82.

76 *Reg. St. Osmund* (Rolls Ser.), i, 234.

77 e.g. ibid. i, 390–1; *Sar. Chart. & Doc.* (Rolls Ser.), 325–8, 333–4, 342–3.

78 Ibid. 325–8, 333–4; *Reg. St. Osmund* (Rolls Ser.), i, 390–1.

79 e.g. *Sar. Chart. & Doc.* (Rolls Ser.), 215–17, 349–51.

80 e.g. ibid. 203–5; cf. *Brit. Arch. Jnl.* 3rd ser. iv, 59, 92–115.

81 e.g. *Sar. Chart. & Doc.* (Rolls Ser.), 326, 350; *Reg. St. Osmund* (Rolls Ser.), i, 392.

82 *Sar. Chart. & Doc.* (Rolls Ser.), 216.

83 Edwards, *Eng. Secular Cath.* 187–93.

84 *Reg. St. Osmund* (Rolls Ser.), ii, 16, 41.

85 *Sar. Chart. & Doc.* (Rolls Ser.), 259–60.

86 T. Walsingham, *Ypodigma Neustriae* (Rolls Ser.), 141; *Eulogium Historiarum* (Rolls Ser.), iii, 118; Matt. Paris, *Chron. Majora* (Rolls Ser.), ii, 407–8; *Close R.* 1237–42, 53, 92, 127, 133–6; *Cal. Pat.* 1232–47, 218, 226, 236.

87 H. Rashdall, *Universities of Europe in the Middle Ages* (1936 edn.), iii, 88–89.

88 *Stat. Sar.* 110–15.

89 See below, p. 369.

90 *Sar. Chart. & Doc.* (Rolls Ser.), 348.

91 *Catalogue Sar. Cath. Libr.* ed. E. M. Thompson and S. M. Lakin, 3, 5, 7, 10–14, 17, 19, 21, 31; Hist. MSS. Com. *Var. Coll.* i, 375–7; *D. and C. Wells*, i, 152; *Oxford Theology and Theologians*, ed. A. G. Little and F. Pelster (Oxf. Hist. Soc.), 253–5.

92 *W.A.M.* l, 230–62, but the account of Salisbury schools is misleading (p. 253).

THE FOURTEENTH CENTURY Towards the end of the 13th and in the 14th centuries there seems to have been a falling away both at the cathedral schools and in some other aspects of cathedral life. Between 1284 and 1297 the quick succession of bishops probably made it difficult to pursue any continuous policy of reform, and Bishop Ghent's register (1297–1315) suggests that he found many abuses to correct both in the diocese and at the cathedral. In 1300 he intervened to administer a sharp rebuke to Master Ralph of York for being the first chancellor since 1240 to neglect his obligation of providing a theological lecturer.[93] By this time the incipient university at Salisbury seems to have disappeared and the cathedral schools, like other English cathedral schools in the later Middle Ages, became of only local significance. Grammar-school masters and theological lecturers were apparently still appointed,[94] though on several occasions the bishop or chapter had to intervene to see that the chancellor did this. About 1350–2 there were difficulties with the aged chancellor, Elias of St. Albans, whose grammar master, Master Henry Nugge, was unsatisfactory and had eventually to be dismissed.[95] Elias also roused the opposition of some members of the chapter by appointing as his theological lecturer, at the request of the Countess of Lancaster, a friar preacher of Salisbury[96] who, doubtless because he had been trained at the Dominican schools instead of at the university, had no degree in theology. On this occasion a compromise was arranged, but eight years later the administration of the theological school was again brought up in chapter. Simon of Sudbury, the chancellor, who was then non-resident, was charged with not having provided a theological lecturer,[97] and in 1358 William de Fornesete, S.T.P., was granted a papal indult for two years' non-residence at his vicarage at Mildenhall, Norwich diocese, while lecturing in theology at Salisbury.[98] In the 14th century apparently neither the chancellors nor other residentiary canons were willing to teach in the theological school as was done in the early 13th century.

The root of the trouble at this time seems to have been the absence of supervision by the dignitaries. Between 1297 and 1379 all six deans were non-resident foreigners.[99] The first, Peter of Savoy, was a kinsman of Edward I; the other five were French or Italian cardinals provided by the popes.[1] In the same period four foreigners were precentors and three cardinals were treasurers, all being papally provided and non-resident. Only the chancellors were English and in five cases out of seven seem to have been resident. Bishop Ghent, Bishop Mortival, and the residentiary members of the chapter made strong protests against these provisions of absentee foreigners, declaring that the dignitaries were intended to be like living cornerstones or pillars of the cathedral, and that their neglect of residence might cause the whole fabric to crash in ruin.[2] Bishop Ghent found to his dismay in 1300 that not only were the dean and precentor absent with papal dispensations, but that the chancellor and treasurer, infected perhaps by their example, were absent without leave. He sternly recalled the chancellor and treasurer, and summoned the dean into residence as soon as his papal dispensation expired.[3] Dean Peter, however, soon secured a further dispensation.[4] In 1311, when a French cardinal, Reymund de Fargis, was provided in his place, the bishop protested but finally agreed to the provision 'out of reverence for the Holy See' and because he was forced by law.[5] Later attempts by Bishop Mortival to compel Cardinal Reymund to reside were unavailing.[6] In 1331 the president and chapter, as a last resort, begged him to procure for them from the Pope a grant of free election to the deanery after his death.[7] At the same time they wrote to their absent treasurer, Cardinal Arnold, deploring the danger to which the rich treasures of the church, the vestments, relics, and ornaments, and especially the bells of great weight and price, were exposed during his absence through the negligence of his officers.[8]

The growth of papal provisions was thus evidently largely responsible for the alarming decrease in the residence of the great dignitaries in the 14th century; but it is more difficult to estimate their results on the residence and personnel of the chapter as a whole. The period when the flood of provisions was greatest at Salisbury was probably between about 1305 and the 1380's, although they can be traced from the time of Bishops Richard Poore and Bingham, when they roused some indignation.[9] They gradually increased throughout the 13th century, but it was not until the early 14th century that Salisbury dignities and archdeaconries were normally given by the popes to absent cardinals,[10] or that provisions to simple prebends were made on a really large scale. Then there is no doubt of their extent and importance. In 1325 Bishop Mortival declared that 28 of the 52 mem-

93 *Reg. Simon de Gandavo* (Cant. & York Soc.), 41–42.

94 e.g. *Cal. Close R.* 1354–60, 508; *W.A.M.* xlviii, 14; E 179/277/8; D. & C. Sar., Reg. Dunham, f. 102.

95 D. & C. Sar., Reg. Corfe, ff. 54, 87.

96 Ibid. f. 38.

97 Ibid. ff. 40, 49, 128.

98 *Cal. Pap. Lett.* 1342–62, 596.

99 See below, p. 208.

1 *Fasti Eccl. Sar*, ed. Jones, lists of dignitaries.

2 D. & C. Sar., Reg. Hemingsby, ff. 42–43; *Reg. Simon de Gandavo* (Cant. & York Soc.), 42–43.

3 *Reg. Simon de Gandavo* (Cant. & York Soc.), 42–43, 160–4.

4 *Cal. Pap. Lett.* 1305–42, 19.

5 *Reg. Simon de Gandavo* (Cant. & York Soc.), 760–2.

6 *W.A.M.* xxi, 161.

7 D. & C. Sar., Reg. Hemingsby, ff. 42–43.

8 Ibid. ff. 43–44.

9 e.g. *Reg. St. Osmund* (Rolls Ser.), ii, 96–100, 388–90; *Sar. Chart. & Doc.* (Rolls Ser.), 260–1; *Cal. Pap. Lett.* 1198–1304, 203.

10 Cf. the lists in *Fasti Eccl. Sar.* ed. Jones.

bers of his chapter had been provided by the popes. These were the dean, an archdeacon, and 6 prebendaries provided by Clement V, and the treasurer, precentor, an archdeacon, and 17 prebendaries provided by John XXII, with 8 more expectant canons awaiting prebends.[11] From the time of Clement V or John XXII provision became the most normal method of appointment to prebends. Fourteen Italian and 11 French cardinals were provided at Salisbury in the 14th century, as compared with only 3 Italian cardinals in the 13th century and 3 in the 15th century.[12] But provisions were no longer confined chiefly to foreigners or to the richer benefices. Increasingly, English royal clerks and university students petitioned the Pope for provisions to Salisbury prebends, and many were successful. The statutes of Provisors and *Praemunire* seem mainly to have given the king greater bargaining power in working out the compromise by which the popes provided large numbers of royal clerks to English benefices in return for the king's acceptance of the provisions of the cardinals. The king's clerks, like the cardinals, usually gained the richer prebends and in most cases were no more resident at the cathedral than the cardinals.[13] But a number of local clergy and university students provided to moderate or poorer prebends in the middle and later decades of the century are known to have entered residence.[14] These, with some prebendaries whom the bishops were still able to collate, formed the core of the residentiary chapter. Possibly, therefore, in this later period, papal provisions were not responsible for so great a decrease in the number of residentiary canons as has sometimes been supposed.

It cannot even be asserted with confidence that the number of residentiaries did decline in the 14th century, for this is the earliest period at which the size of the residentiary body can be estimated with any accuracy. From about 1329, except for the abnormal plague years around 1350, the new evidence of the chapter act books and a few quarterly communar account rolls shows that about twelve or fourteen canons normally made their full residence in each quarter of the year;[15] sometimes, towards the end of the century, when the dignitaries again began to enter residence, there were considerably more. Such evidence as has survived from the 13th century suggests that the rota of 1215 failed to work satisfactorily from the start[16] and by 1319 changes were urgently needed in the statutes to make them more conformable with existing custom. Therefore Bishop Mortival and his chapter made it clear that in future a canon might choose any one quarter or parts of all four quarters of the year in which to complete his three months' residence; and so long as he earned 40*s.* in daily commons during the year, which he could do by attending the cathedral services for twelve days less than the full three months, he was to be legally exempt from the fine of a fifth imposed on the non-residents.[17] This concession might be expected to have resulted in the presence of fewer canons in the close at all times as well as in the residence of unequal numbers at different times of the year.

In practice, however, neither of these results seems to have ensued. It appears that about eight to eleven canons were in residence nearly all the year round, attending chapter meetings at all periods of the year and usually earning more than their 40*s.* commons in each quarter throughout the century. The remaining two or three residentiaries might be present only for about three to six months. These were usually diocesan officials, household clerks of the Bishop of Salisbury or of other bishops, university masters or students, or men who were also residentiaries of the neighbouring cathedral of Wells.[18] A growing distinction between the two bodies of residentiary and non-residentiary canons, which the statutes of 1215 had been unable to check, was emphasized by the various conditions and obligations now imposed on those who decided to profess residence. The imposition of the fine on the non-residents had in fact made residence legally optional. It then became customary for a canon wishing to reside to be formally admitted to residence in chapter. At the same time he was required to pay 40*s.* as security that he would provide an entrance feast for the bishop, canons and lesser cathedral clergy at his house in the close.[19] In 1319 Bishop Mortival, alarmed at the excessive outlay on such feasts, ordered that no canon might spend on them more than the annual value of his prebend, and that any canon might pay a fine of £40 to the cathedral fabric instead of giving a feast.[20] Most canons in the early 14th century preferred to pay the fine, and in this way an entrance fee for residence was gradually substituted for feasting. The chapter's object in making these conditions was probably that it felt the need of some pledge of a canon's purpose to reside in return for admitting him to share in the increasingly valuable distributions from the common fund and to a canonical house

[11] Sar. Reg. Mortival, ii, f. 215 (234).

[12] C. Moor, 'Cardinals beneficed in Salisbury Cathedral', *W.A.M.* l, 136–48.

[13] Cf. the 1366 returns of pluralists in *Reg. Langham* (Cant. & York Soc.), i, 1–109; *Reg. Sudbury* (Cant. & York Soc.), ii, 148–82.

[14] e.g. Master John Wilton, a former de Vaux scholar, obtained the £5 Stratford prebend in 1349/51 by papal provision, and became a residentiary: *Cal. Pap. Lett.* 1342–62, 361; *Cal. Pap. Pet.* 1342–1419, 205–6; D. & C. Sar. Reg. Corfe, f. 66; Communar's Acct. R. 1369.

[15] Edwards, *Eng. Secular Cath.* 77–81.

[16] *Stat. Sar.* 70–73, 88–91, 160–1.

[17] Ibid. 160–1.

[18] Edwards, *Eng. Secular Cath.* 79–82.

[19] Records of admissions to residence and payments of 40*s.* pledges and of fines in place of feasting are in the earliest chapter act books: D. & C. Sar., Reg. Hemingsby, ff. 3, 85, 96; Reg. Corfe, f. 19. For a possible origin of the 40*s.* see *Stat. Sar.* 61.

[20] *Stat. Sar.* 144–7.

in the close. There seems little evidence that in the 14th century the residentiaries at Salisbury were deliberately trying to restrict residence to as few canons as possible in order to keep larger shares of the common fund for themselves. It was, however, natural that a canon who went to the expense of paying his entrance fee and acquiring a house would want to settle down in it. Thus the residentiaries came gradually to form a close inner chapter, controlling the cathedral administration, while the non-residents became more detached from cathedral affairs, attending perhaps only a few general chapters. Only the occasional presence of a few residentiaries making their short statutory residence in the intervals of other work may have helped to retard this development.

A more obvious way in which the 14th century at Salisbury seems to mark a decline is in the deterioration of the relations between bishop and chapter. This was not apparent in the pontificates of Simon of Ghent and Roger Mortival, but, from 1330, all the 14th-century bishops of Salisbury were civil servants provided by the popes in collaboration with the royal government. The chapter still went through the form of obtaining a royal *congé d'élire*, and, in two cases at least, held an election, which was then quashed on grounds that the see had previously been reserved, and the royal nominee was provided.[21] Naturally the chapter was less ready to welcome these bishops than canons whom they themselves had chosen, while the bishops were less sympathetic to the chapter's rights and privileges than their predecessors, and more anxious to assert their own authority. All the bishops, however, gave prebends to certain of their kinsmen or members of their households and so gradually acquired influence in the chapter. Some members of the chapter continued to act as bishop's commissaries and officials in the diocese. At the time when there was friction between the chapter and Bishop Wyville, the chapter approved the bishop's plan to reunite Sherborne castle to the bishopric, and went surety with him to the Earl of Salisbury to the amount of £10,000 for it;[22] and, at the peak of the great quarrel with Bishop Waltham, certain residentiary canons continued to act as his councillors even though, as members of the chapter, they were strongly opposing his claims to jurisdiction at the cathedral. Possibly there is a certain artificiality about some of these quarrels. Many of the residentiary canons were lawyers, willing and almost eager to continue the long negotiations and lawsuits for indefinite periods. At the same time the bishops, determined though they were to assert their claims, were ready to recognize that 'a cathedral church and college could not exist unless it had privileges and customs'.[23] As a result, many outstanding disputes about jurisdiction were settled, and the age was one of definition and compromise.

The results of this definition were by no means always favourable to the chapter although in some cases they were. For example, Bishop Wyville's and Bishop Erghum's attempts to exercise jurisdiction in the vacant deanery were decisively defeated, and the chapter's victory was registered in the composition of 1392, which said that all profits and jurisdiction of the vacant deanery were in future to belong fully to the chapter.[24] This was important, because exercise of the decanal jurisdiction in a vacancy would have made the bishop immediate ordinary of the cathedral church and of the prebendal churches and estates, which the chapter insisted were normally subject to his correction only through the dean. The chapter also objected to Bishop Wyville coming to their meetings and claiming a share in the daily distributions of the common fund when present at the cathedral.[25] The bishop had been a canon and prebendary, with the right to sit in chapter, since Osmund's time, and Bishop Wyville maintained his claims. The really big quarrel, however, arose when Bishop Erghum and Bishop Waltham revived the claims to episcopal visitation surrendered by Bishop Bridport.[26] This quarrel lasted for thirteen years, during which successive appeals were made to Canterbury and Rome and proctors were maintained at Rome at the chapter's expense, until finally the king intervened to secure peace. In the meantime many lesser disputes had inflamed the relations of bishop and chapter. Most of them were settled in the composition of 1392 confirmed by Pope Boniface,[27] and the chapter gained some concessions. But the most important clauses were those which laid down that in future bishops of Salisbury could visit their cathedral church once in seven years. The visitation was not to last longer than five days, and the bishop was tied to a certain procedure, but the settlement was a severe blow to the chapter's privileged position.

Thus in the 14th century the chapter suffered at least three major losses of privileges and independence: the loss in practice of its right to elect its bishop and dean, and the loss of its exemption from episcopal visitation. Yet the period was not solely one of loss; at the same time there were forward moves. One of these was the issue by Bishop Mortival in 1319 of the important set of statutes, which attempted to review the whole field of cathedral legislation.[28] It comprised 48

[21] *Cal. Pat.* 1327–30, 498, 531–3; 1374–7, 168, 208; 1391–6, 633, 664; *Cal. Close* 1330–3, 156; Sar. Reg. Waltham, ff. 1–5; Sar. Reg. Metford, ff. 1–2; *Rot. Parl.* (Rec. Com.), iii, 460.

[22] D. & C. Sar., Reg. Hemingsby, f. 86; cf. *Cal. Close*, 1354–60, 180, 190.

[23] D. & C. Sar., Reg. Dunham, f. 72.

[24] *Stat. Sar.* 302–5; D. & C. Sar., Reg. Hemingsby, ff. 71–72, 112–13, 133–40; Reg. Coman, f. 72; Reg. Dunham, ff. 18–20.

[25] D. & C. Sar., Reg. Corfe, f. 111.

[26] Ibid. Reg. Coman, ff. 69–77; Reg. Dunham, ff. 3, 18–20, 53–58, 72–74, 77, 80–83, 106–7, 109, 133–4, 138–9, 168, 178–82, 193, 198–9.

[27] *Stat. Sar.* 282–307.

[28] Ibid. 134–275.

chapters grouped into eleven sections. Beginning with the canons and their residence, it continued with rules for the conduct of chapter business, the care of the common property and the cathedral fabric, and the duties of dignitaries, to the vicars choral, liturgical changes, and the choristers. The arrangement is not so logical as these headings suggest, for many things appear in unexpected places. Moreover, no subject is dealt with comprehensively in the manner of a code of statutes. Knowledge and use of St. Osmund's Institution, the Consuetudinary, and other earlier statutes were assumed. Where their rulings were still useful they were emphasized, and where obsolete revised, as in the case of canonical residence. At the same time some important new laws were made, as for example in the union of the office of penitentiary with that of sub-dean, and the imposition of obligations of continual residence on the sub-dean and succentor, whose offices were doubtless more essential now that the dean and precentor were frequently absent. The spirit of the work was that of the reformer, and Bishop Mortival tells us that he alone was not responsible. His predecessor, Simon of Ghent, had planned the work and summoned a full congregation of canons to discuss it, but had died before it could be completed. Bishop Mortival carried it out with the collaboration of the chapter, and the resulting constitutions were issued by the unanimous decision of all. The authority of these statutes is still recognized at Salisbury in so far as they do not conflict with later changes or the new statutes of 1937,[29] and until they were, with the Institution and the Consuetudinary, the most obvious and complete source of information for the chapter's constitution. They seem to have had less influence on the statutes of other English secular cathedrals than the Institution or the Consuetudinary, although some traces of their influence are found in the statutes compiled for Lincoln Cathedral in 1440.[30]

In the steady growth of the influence of the Use of Salisbury throughout Canterbury province the work of the 14th-century chapter was vital. Many additions had already been made to the Salisbury Ordinal since the early 13th century, incorporating changes of custom, new feasts and octaves, and greater accuracy in directions.[31] In 1319 Bishop Mortival in his statutes ordered further alterations,[32] and the period between 1319 and 1337 was one of especial activity when an important set of marginal additions was made to the 13th-century text.[33] These were the stepping-stones to a new ordinal, the 'Ordinal Wellwyk', which was probably compiled before 1350 by Thomas de Welewick, precentor from 1341 to 1343.[34] This ordinal was largely responsible for the growing popularity and adoption of the 'new' Salisbury Use outside the diocese in the late 14th century. It formed the necessary link with the 15th-century liturgical work and made possible its startling success.

The 14th-century residentiary chapter also seems to have devoted much time and thought to keeping administrative records. The series of chapter act books recording the minutes of chapter meetings dates from 1329 and probably resulted from an order in Bishop Mortival's statutes in 1319 that for the future a faithful record of all chapter business was to be kept by a sworn notary appointed by the chapter, since 'when there are no written minutes, people make contradictory assertions about matters discussed in their presence'.[35] A system of chronological entries was soon adopted, and the minutes were fully and carefully written.[36] At the same time it was decided to elect annually a residentiary canon as *Custos Munimentorum*, to be responsible for the safe keeping of all the chapter's muniments.[37] As a result many more documents have survived from this period than from earlier times. The general impression gained from study of these records is one of careful and efficient administration. There were some rather petty quarrels among the residentiaries, and the chapter, in the absence of the dean and most of the other dignitaries, had a difficult task in disciplining the lesser clergy, yet it was very persistent, painstaking, and anxious to settle disputes and enforce discipline in strict accordance with law and precedent. Vicars choral and chantry chaplains were constantly summoned before the dean's *locum tenens* or the president and chapter to answer for neglect of their duties; for coming late to cathedral services and leaving early; for chattering in choir; for playing ball in the close; for wearing a belt of marvellous size, a cape of many colours, or boots of red and green squares, unsuitable to clerks in holy orders; for going off to Southampton for the day in a striped costume, carrying arms; for quarrelling, brawling, and frequenting city taverns; for entertaining strangers and lay people, especially women, in their houses in the close, and for incontinence.[38] Normally they were rebuked, fined, and warned; some, found incorrigible after many warnings, were dismissed and deprived of their benefices.

The vicars choral were undoubtedly a turbulent element in the 14th-century close. They outnumbered the residentiary canons by about four or five to one, and they included priests holding responsible offices at the cathedral, such as clerk of the fabric, sub-communar, and sub-treasurer, as

29 *Lond. Gaz.* Order in Council, 8 June 1937.
30 W. H. Frere, *Use Sar.* i, xxii, xxxvii.
31 Ibid. ii, xii–xvii.
32 *Stat. Sar.* 246–9.
33 *Use Sar.* ii, xviii–xxi.
34 Ibid. xx–xxvi.
35 *Stat. Sar.* 166–9.
36 At first experiments were made in entering them on blank leaves of the chapter's cartulary, *Liber Evidenciarum C*; then separate registers were used named after the chapter notary who wrote them. These are extant from 1329 (with gaps 1358–85, 1476–97, and 1642–60) until the date of writing (1954).
37 *Stat. Sar.* 168–71.
38 D. & C. Sar., Reg. Hemingsby, Corfe, Coman, Dunham, *passim.*

well as young men who were still supposed to be attending the chancellor's grammar school. A demand for greater corporate independence seems to have developed among them, especially in the early 14th century. In 1319 Bishop Mortival and the chapter told the vicars roundly that 'the servant is not greater than his lord', and ordered all statutes which suggested equality between canons and vicars to be utterly revoked.[39] In spite of this Bishop Mortival was a generous benefactor to the vicars. On his death in 1330 he left instructions that any residue from his estate was to be used to purchase some permanent endowment to give each vicar ½*d.* a day more than his customary payment from the church.[40] Already in 1317 the vicars had themselves obtained a general licence from the king to acquire property in mortmain to the value of £40 a year, so that each might receive an additional ½*d.* a day,[41] but so far their only acquisition under this licence had been a small estate in Boscombe, valued at 40*s.* a year.[42] With £500 eventually paid over by Bishop Mortival's executors, the dean and chapter bought the patronage of West Hanney church (Berks.), valued at £40 a year, and arranged for its appropriation to the vicars' maintenance.[43] In 1392 licence was granted for the alienation in mortmain to the dean and chapter for the vicars of six shops in Salisbury and the reversion of Stotton Manor in Upway (Dors.), valued together at £20 a year.[44]

By this time the flow of gifts to the chapter had practically dried up, apart from endowments given for the foundation of chantries and obits. The last important addition to the common fund was Winkfield church (Berks.), acquired from Abingdon Abbey in 1308.[45] For the rest of the century there were some very small annual pensions granted by religious houses in return for the chapter's consent to the appropriation of churches to them.[46] In the 14th century there was probably little need to increase the endowments of the common fund or of the dignities and prebends, but the fabric and its revenues caused more anxiety. Storms and floods in the early 14th century raised fears for the cathedral's foundations, which the chapter's desire for water had caused to be laid in marshy ground. Bishop Mortival appealed for help to the laity, but their devotion to the cathedral was said to be growing cold, and they preferred to found private oratories.[47] By 1363 the walls and belfry were cracked and falling, and the bishop and chapter petitioned the Pope for permission to appropriate St. Thomas's Church, Salisbury, in the bishop's collation, to the fabric fund. This was allowed for six years only.[48] In 1366 the dean and chapter purchased a general licence to acquire in mortmain further property to the value of £20 a year for the fabric.[49] By the end of the century they had obtained lands in Erlestoke and Boreham by Bishopstrow; rents in Salisbury given by the treasurer, John Chandler, and the permanent appropriation of St. Thomas's Church.[50]

Throughout the century the residentiary canons took an active part in the administration of the chapter's property. No such general change can be traced from direct management of the common estates to leasing as happened at monasteries in the later Middle Ages, for the chapter as a corporation lived on rents payable by its own members from an early period. Existing custom was set out in Bishop Mortival's statutes of 1319. Farms of the chapter's common estates and churches were granted as 'options' to the residentiary canons according to their seniority in residence, for old-established and settled quarterly rents,[51] which were probably then well below the actual value of the property. Chapter farms were an important part of the profits of residence, and there was much competition for them. Eight days after a residentiary's death, his farm was offered in chapter as an 'option' to the remaining residentiaries.[52] If it were a profitable farm desired by a senior residentiary, this would lead to a general post in farms, each residentiary in turn resigning his farm in order to accept one resigned by his senior in residence. When estates lay very near the cathedral, as in the case of Britford, a residentiary may have managed them himself, through bailiffs or members of his household;[53] in other cases he may have leased them to a sub-farmer, who doubtless paid him a higher rent than that which went to the chapter. A clerk sub-farmer, who acted under two successive canon farmers, has been found at Hilton in 1348, and a layman at Melksham in 1358.[54]

The residentiaries as a body assumed responsibility for the general supervision of both the common property and the prebends. Once in three years two or three canons were appointed by the residentiary chapter to visit all the common property at the common expense to survey defects and estimate the cost of repairs.[55] Such surveys might also be requested for particular estates at other times by in-going or out-going canon-farmers or prebendaries in order to settle their responsibility for repairs, but in these cases were made at their

39 *Stat. Sar.* 242–5.
40 *W.A.M.* xlviii, 205–7.
41 *Cal. Pat.* 1313–17, 654; *Stat. Sar.* 320 n. where it is misdated.
42 *Cal. Pat.* 1317–21, 496.
43 Ibid. 1350–4, 270; *Cal. Pap. Pet.* 1342–1419, 235; *Cal. Pap. Lett.* 1342–62, 511.
44 *Cal. Pat.* 1391–6, 124.
45 Ibid. 1307–13, 55.
46 e.g. D. & C. Sar., Reg. Corfe, f. 130; Reg. Coman, f. 55; Reg. Dunham, f. 1; Reg. Holme, f. 46; *Cal. Pap. Lett.* 1362–1404, 89; 1396–1404, 162–3, 246–7, 327–9, 354.
47 *Stat. Sar.* 194–201.
48 *Cal. Pap. Lett.* 1362–1404, 89.
49 *Cal. Pat.* 1364–7, 314.
50 Ibid. 1391–6, 97, 300; 1396–9, 573–4; 1399–1401, 392; *Cal. Pap. Lett.* 1396–1404, 474.
51 *Stat. Sar.* 188–9.
52 Ibid. 280–1. The assignment of farms is entered regularly in the chapter act books.
53 D. & C. Sar., Reg. Corfe, f. 68.
54 Ibid. ff. 8, 134.
55 *Stat. Sar.* 190–1. The act books show that this statute was carried out.

expense.[56] The individual canons were normally responsible for repairs on their farms as on their prebends, though, if new buildings were needed, the cost was borne by the chapter.[57] In the 14th century some prebends, particularly of the non-resident aliens, were also leased for sums considerably greater than their assessed *verus valor*.[58] Some residentiary canons were apparently ready to accept leases of the Wiltshire and Dorset prebends and to profit from them. John Gough, for example, a king's clerk and residentiary about the middle of the century, obtained a lease of the estates of an alien dignitary, of some common property needing special supervision, and of his own chapter farm.[59] The many civil and canon lawyers among the residentiaries would doubtless have knowledge of the laws of property and estate management. They, with the chapter notaries and other cathedral clergy, were able to conduct most of the chapter's legal business without the help of outside lawyers, such as the religious houses now usually employed. In fact, residentiary canons of Salisbury are often found in the 14th century acting in this capacity for religious houses or for lay and ecclesiastical magnates of the diocese.[60]

In the 14th century more chantry masses were founded in the cathedral than in any other period. Fourteen chantry foundations have been traced[61] in addition to the nine or ten dating from the late 12th and 13th centuries, while lists of obit distributions suggest that between 40 and 50 obits were also being celebrated annually.[62] As in the earlier period, most of the founders were bishops or canons of Salisbury, with a few city clergy and laity. Roger Clone, Archdeacon of Dorset, provided his chantry chaplain with a small house in the close annexed to his office,[63] and three chantries, those of Bishop Ghent and of two canons, Henry Blunsdon, Edward I's almoner, and John Gough, were for two chaplains each. Some chantries were intended to support perpetual chaplains appointed for life; others, usually the less adequately endowed, were for stipendiary priests or vicars choral appointed annually. In 1319 Bishop Mortival and his chapter discouraged the granting of the perpetual chantries to vicars choral,[64] but the small stipends of both chaplains and vicars probably made his order impracticable. In 1390 there were apparently only seven chantry chaplains at the cathedral who were not also vicars choral.[65] The chapter drew up an annual table of *missae currentes*, arranging that those chaplains who were not also vicars choral should celebrate their daily masses successively at the different cathedral altars, so that there should always be a mass which workmen, travellers, or other passers-by could attend from dawn until 10 or 11 a.m.[66] If one chaplain did not begin his mass immediately the preceding chaplain had finished, he was cited before the chapter for neglect of duty. Thus the chantry masses formed an important addition to the cathedral services. Moreover, the chaplains were expected to take part in the main cathedral services, especially on feasts of nine lessons, and were subject to the dean and chapter's direction and discipline in much the same way as the vicars choral.[67] Several of them held cathedral offices, such as clerk of the works, sub-communar, or master of the choristers.

Another group of cathedral clergy made necessary by the chantries were the altarists, who served the cathedral altars, helping the chantry priests, and being responsible for the altars' furniture. By the late 14th century there were six senior altarists, known as *altaristae intrinseci* or *altaristae antiqui*, who were apparently attached to altars in the inner choir, while three *altaristae extrinseci* were probably attached to altars in the outer choir or nave.[68] They were supposed to report to the chapter any chaplain or vicar choral who failed to say his mass at the proper time; they served as acolytes at the high altar for the high mass, and two or three *altaristae extrinseci* were also known as the sacrists' boys and had to help in cleaning the church and in the bell-ringing.[69] Their salaries might extend to 36*s.* 4*d.* a year,[70] some of it deriving from the chantry endowments, supplemented by payments from the treasurer and the common fund, and by invitation to meals from the residentiary canons. Apparently they were normally chosen from former choristers whose voices had broken.[71]

One of the most interesting developments at the 14th-century cathedral was the provision made for housing and teaching the choristers. Here there was a very definite advance on the arrangements of earlier times, when the choristers had been subject only to the precentor's general supervision and discipline. They had had no certain food or lodging, and were said to have gone from door to door

[56] *Stat. Sar.* 184–7, 276–9.

[57] Ibid. 182–7, 190–1.

[58] e.g. *Cal. Fine R.* 1347–56, 182, 198–9; 1369–77, 317.

[59] D. & C. Sar., Reg. Corfe, ff. 127, 134; *Cal. Fine R.* 1347–56, 323.

[60] e.g. *Cal. Close* 1349–54, 510; 1360–4, 317, 330; 1364–8, 314; 1374–7, 459; 1385–9, 617, 620; *Cal. Pat.* 1396–9, 447; *Cat. Anct. D.* iii, C. 31712 (p. 401).

[61] *Cal. Pat.* 1313–17, 98–99, 159; 1330–4, 434; 1334–8, 47, 344; 1340–3, 346–7; 1354–8, 46, 149, 157, 341, 347; 1358–61, 125; 1361–4, 38, 155, 237, 439; 1364–7, 166, 314; 1391–6, 300; D. & C. Sar., Reg. Corfe, ff. 45–46, 71; Press I, Box Sar. Roger Clone's chart. 1369; Sar. Reg. Neville, f. 49; *Valor Eccl.* (Rec. Com.), ii, 81.

[62] D. & C. Sar., Communar's acct. rolls.

[63] D. & C. Sar., Press I, Box Sar. Roger Clone's chart. 1369.

[64] *Stat. Sar.* 258–9.

[65] Lamb. Reg. Courtenay, f. 149.

[66] *Stat. Sar.* 258–61; *Ceremonies and Processions, Sar.* 198, 224–8.

[67] *Stat. Sar.* 254–7; D. & C. Sar., Reg. Dunham, ff. 262–3.

[68] D. & C. Sar, Reg. Dunham, ff. 7–8, 130; Reg. Hemingsby, f. 144; Reg. Burgh, f. 24; Reg. Newton, ff. 31–32; Lamb. Reg. Courtenay, f. 149; *Stat. Sar.* 379–80 n.; *Ceremonies and Processions, Sar.* 155–6, 228 n.

[69] *Ceremonies and Processions, Sar.* 155–6; *Stat. Sar.* 307 n., 379–80 n.

[70] *Stat. Sar.* 307.

[71] D. & C. Sar., Reg. Dunham, ff. 7–8.

of the canons' houses, begging bread; and had no master to keep them out of mischief.[72] The solution of Bishop Ghent and Bishop Mortival was to endow a boarding house for them, administered by the dean and chapter. In 1314 Bishop Ghent gave rents in Salisbury for the support of fourteen choristers and a master to teach them grammar,[73] and in 1322 Bishop Mortival gave Preshute church (and later 100*s.* annual pension from West Hanney church (Berks.)), and arranged for the boys to live together in a house in the close.[74] There was to be no more begging and the boys were to devote themselves to the cathedral services and study under the supervision of a submaster. A residentiary canon was to be elected by the chapter as their warden to administer their revenues and to appoint the sub-master, who might be a vicar choral or chantry chaplain. The boys were to be formally admitted by the dean and chapter and their appointment was not left entirely to the precentor. The boy bishop and his attendants were no longer to be allowed their visitation and feasting on Holy Innocents Day, though they might execute their offices in the church and go to dinner at a canon's house afterwards provided that they returned to school and church the next day.[75] In 1346 complaints were made about their food by three vicars acting as spokesmen for the boys: two loaves were brought as samples to the chapter house, where the canons pronounced them 'good enough'.[76] In 1395 Bishop Waltham left the boys 6*s.* 8*d.* a year and their submaster 2*s.* a year for chanting a daily antiphon of the Virgin before the high altar after compline for his soul.[77]

THE END OF THE MIDDLE AGES

Towards the end of the 14th and in the early 15th centuries there was a remarkable revival of cathedral life. Among the immediate causes and signs of it were the return of the great dignitaries to residence, and the end of the long dispute between bishop and chapter by the award of 1392. The change in the dignitaries resulted from the papal schism and the attitude to it of the English government. When Parliament took the side of Urban VI all the Salisbury dignities and prebends of the French cardinals supporting Clement VII were confiscated. In 1380 and 1381 Urban repeopled the College of Cardinals and provided them to rich English benefices: but there was much opposition from Parliament. The treasury of Salisbury and the archdeaconries of Dorset and Berkshire were given to cardinals,[78] but all provisions to the deanery were refused. The last foreign Dean of Salisbury, James of Orsini, an Italian cardinal, died in 1379, and the chapter was allowed to exercise its right of election.[79] In 1381, after the provision of Dean Robert Braybrook to the bishopric of London, the Pope again reserved the deanery and provided to it two Italian cardinals in succession. Neither, however, gained posession, and the deanery was held without difficulty by Thomas Montagu, a kinsman of the Earl of Salisbury, regularly elected by the chapter.[80] The protests of Parliament against the other cardinals became stronger, and by 1384–5 they also had been replaced by Englishmen.[81] In the 1390's an increasing number of civil servants, *generosi*, and bishops' kinsmen drew their incomes from Salisbury dignities and prebends.[82] By the end of the century all four principal dignitaries were in residence together and the residentiaries numbered about fifteen.[83] The formal entry of Dean Montagu into residence took place in 1390,[84] when the chapter's quarrel with Bishop Waltham was at its height. This dean had already been active in summoning general chapters of both residentiary and non-resident canons to take counsel and to grant taxes from their prebends to pay for the chapter's lawsuits and for the repair of the tower and spire.[85] Then, after the award of 1392, as the first episcopal visitation approached, a great overhaul of the cathedral's administration began under his direction. The vicars choral, chantry chaplains, and choristers were rebuked, corrected, and reminded of their duties; surveys were made of the chapter's farms and prebends; inventories were drawn up of the library and muniments; the statutes were viewed and in some cases revised; the ornaments and furniture of the altars were inspected.[86] When Bishop Waltham finally came in 1394 he claimed to have found some faults, but only minor ones were specified in his formal letters to the chapter.[87]

By the early 15th century the chapter had become one of the most distinguished ecclesiastical bodies of the later Middle Ages, comparable in the learning, statesmanship, and administrative ability

72 *Cal. Pat.* 1327–30, 487–8; Sar. Reg. Mortival, ii, 265–7; D. H. Robertson, *Sarum Close*, 40–43.

73 *Cal. Pat.* 1313–17, 112, and see *V.C.H. Wilts.* v.

74 *Cal. Pat.* 1317–21, 567–8; 1327–30, 487–8; 1350–4, 270; *Cal. Pap. Pet.* 1342–1419, 235; *Cal. Pap. Lett.* 1342–62, 511; Sar. Reg. Mortival, i, 195*b*; ii, 141–3, 151*a*, 265–7; *W.A.M.* xlviii, 201–8; Robertson, *Sarum Close*, 40–43; *Stat. Sar.* 262–7.

75 *Stat. Sar.* 262–7; for the boy bishop at Salisbury see Robertson, op. cit. 78–94.

76 D. & C. Sar., Reg. Hemingsby, f. 120.

77 D. & C. Sar., Reg. Holme, f. 10; Press III, Box Choristers (23).

78 E. Perroy, *L'Angleterre et le Grand Schisme d'Occident*, 54–62, 272–3, 282–3.

79 Sar. Reg. Erghum, i, 33*b*; *Cal. Pap. Lett.* 1362–1404, 401.

80 *Cal. Pap. Lett.* 1362–1404, 335–6, 401; *Cal. Pat.* 1381–5, 237; 1391–6, 566; E. Perroy, op. cit., 283.

81 Perroy, op. cit., 283–5; lists in *Fasti Eccl. Sar.*

82 *W.A.M.* li, 484.

83 D. & C. Sar., Communars' Acct. R. 1398, 1399.

84 Ibid. Reg. Dunham, ff. 141–2.

85 Ibid. Reg. Coman, ff. 69–77. *Campanile* here and on pp. 178 and 182 probably means tower and spire, not the detached belfry: cf. W. Dodsworth, *Sar. Cath. Ch.* 157–62 and *Acts of P.C.* 1422–9, 37.

86 Ibid. Reg. Dunham, ff. 257–71.

87 Ibid. ff. 272, 275–6, 290–1; Sar. Reg. Waltham, pt. iii, 42–43.

of its members to the chapter of the early 13th century. This cannot be attributed solely to the wise appointments of canons by its outstanding bishops, Robert Hallam and John Chandler, for the revival had begun earlier in Dean Montagu's time, and many of the leading members of the early 15th-century chapter had been appointed before 1400. Master John Chandler, the Wykehamist, a leading spirit in the reform movement from the first, was a king's clerk, who obtained his first prebend at Salisbury by 1388 and the treasurership by papal provision in 1394.[88] Hallam became a prebendary in 1395.[89] The chancellor, Master Walter Metford, later Dean of Wells, and Master Henry Chichele, the future Archbishop of Canterbury, owed their promotion to Bishop Metford, Richard II's secretary.[90] Master William Loring, a brother of the Black Prince's steward Sir Niel Loring, both a lawyer and a theologian, a fellow of Merton College, Oxford, and a benefactor of both Merton College and Cambridge University Libraries, was already a senior residentiary in 1395.[91] Master Adam Mottram, the archbishop's chancellor and Archdeacon of Canterbury, entered residence as precentor in 1397.[92] Master Simon Sydenham, the future dean, and Master Robert Brown were members of the chapter by 1404–5.[93] The appointment of Master Richard Ullerston, Chancellor of Oxford University, and author of a treatise petitioning for reforms at the General Council of Pisa, was, however, due to Bishop Hallam, as were those of Master John Fyton, Master Roger Basset, Master William Clynt, John Luke, and others who had taken part under his leadership in the Councils of Pisa and Constance.[94] After Hallam's death in 1417, Bishop Chandler seems to have continued collating men with conciliar experience to Salisbury prebends.[95]

The interest and share of members of Salisbury chapter in these great councils of Christendom are remarkable. Probably they were greater than anywhere else in England except the universities. In 1414 the chapter appointed four of its canons (two residentiaries and two non-residents) to attend the Council of Constance as its special proctors,[96] and is the only English chapter known to have done this. About a quarter of the whole English delegation to Constance was in some way connected with the chapter, either as canons or as members of its confraternity.[97] In the debates at the Council the chief figures of Salisbury, Bishop Hallam, Bishop Bubwith, Thomas Polton, and Henry Chichele, stood out. The sermons and leadership of Bishop Hallam gave firmness and moral purpose to their proposals for reform and unity.[98] Moreover, the chapter at home apparently shared its bishop's conciliar enthusiasm. A sermon preached by Master Richard of Ullerston before a general chapter of residentiary and non-resident canons in 1416 began with a special bidding prayer for the happy issue of the Council, for their bishop absent there, for his contribution to the unity of the universal church, and for the Emperor Sigismund and Henry V.[99]

Doubtless the position of Bishop Hallam as leader of the English nation at Constance had much to do with this interest at Salisbury. The chapter was also alive to any opportunity for urging the canonization of St. Osmund in the counsels of the universal church. The plan for the canonization was put forward as early as 1387 in a sermon by Master Thomas Southam to a general chapter summoned by Dean Montagu.[1] Bishop Erghum had not welcomed it,[2] but John Chandler was appointed to take letters from the chapter to king and Pope urging the canonization,[3] and in 1389 a group of distinguished and influential laymen and women, including John of Gaunt, Constance his wife, Henry, Earl of Derby, his son, with Sir Thomas Percy, Bigot, Blount, and many other knights, ladies, and clerks of their households were admitted to the chapter's confraternity.[4] In return for sharing in the spiritual benefits of the chapter's prayers, these *confratres* and *sorores* might be able to promote the canonization at the papal court.[5] Moreover, a distinguished confraternity increased the chapter's prestige and influence. A second determined effort to secure the canonization was made in Bishop Hallam's pontificate. The bishop and chapter petitioned the Pope, while Dean Chandler held another general chapter at which the entrance fees of the residentiaries and a tax of a tenth on the incomes of all prebends for seven years were voted for the expenses of the canonization and of the cathedral fabric.[6] At this chapter the object of popularizing the Salisbury liturgy was clearly linked with the canonization in Richard of Ullerston's sermon, which claimed that

88 D. & C. Sar., Reg. Coman, f. 77; *Cal. Pap. Lett.* 1362–1404, 289; *Reg. Chichele* (Cant. & York Soc.), ii, 645.

89 *Fasti Eccl. Sar.* ed. Jones, 366.

90 Ibid. 338; *W.A.M.* li, 488–9.

91 D. & C. Sar., Reg. Holme, f. 10; for his career see *Reg. Chichele* (Cant. & York Soc.), ii, 662; *W.A.M.* li, 490.

92 *Reg. Chichele* (Cant. & York Soc.), ii, 666; D. & C. Sar., Reg. Holme, ff. 80–81, 87.

93 *Fasti Eccl. Sar.* ed. Jones, 149, 414.

94 Ibid. 355, 387, 392, 408, 414; D. & C. Sar., Reg. Pountney, ff. 40, 43–4; E. F. Jacob, *Essays in Conciliar Epoch*, 79–82; *W.A.M.* li, 491–2; C. M. D. Crowder, 'English Nation at Council of Constance' (Oxf. D.Phil. thesis, 1953).

95 e.g. Robert Gilbert and John Stokes: D. & C. Sar., Reg. Pountney, f. 95; *Fasti Eccl. Sar.* ed. Jones, 399.

96 D. & C. Sar., Reg. Pountney, f. 8.

97 C. M. D. Crowder, 'Engl. Nation at Constance' (Oxf. D.Phil. thesis, 1953).

98 E. F. Jacob, *Essays in Conciliar Epoch*, 76; *W.A.M.* li, 479, 490–1.

99 *Canonization of St. Osmund*, ed. A. R. Malden, 236 sqq.

1 D. & C. Sar., Reg. Coman, ff. 70–73.

2 Ibid. f. 77; *Canonization of St. Osmund*, ed. A. R. Malden, p. iv.

3 D. & C. Sar., Reg. Coman, f. 77.

4 Ibid. Reg. Dunham, f. 117; *Ceremonies and Processions, Sar.*, 146–7.

5 e.g. *Canonization of St. Osmund*, ed. A. R. Malden, 94–96.

6 Ibid. pp. iv–v; D. & C. Sar., Reg. Pountney, ff. 49–52.

Osmund's composition of the Use of Salisbury, 'incomparable in the world', was, with his saintly life, his miracles, and his foundation of the chapter, a main reason for his canonization.[7] Doubtless the chapter also hoped that the offerings at a saint's shrine would help to repair the cathedral fabric, particularly the tower and spire, which had long been in a precarious state, and was now declared to be ruinous.[8] For the time being, however, the expenses of the canonization put a heavy burden on the chapter. In 1428 the entrance fee for residentiaries was raised from £40 to £100 and 100*s.* for dignitaries, and 100 marks and 100*s.* for simple canons, from which one-fifth was to be applied to St. Osmund's *bursa* and one-fifth to the fabric.[9] Altogether the canonization cost the chapter £731 13*s.*, of which £419 13*s.* was raised by taxation, £312 advanced on loan;[10] and successive residentiary canons and chapter clerks spent weary years at the papal court pressing on the negotiations. The busiest periods were about 1424, when the papal judges-delegate began to examine the evidence for Osmund's miracles, life, and work; about 1442–4, when Master Andrew Holles, the chancellor, and Master Nicholas Upton, the precentor, were active in Rome with Master Simon Houchyns, the chapter clerk and former fellow of de Vaux college; and from 1452, when the new bishop, Richard Beauchamp, entered with vigour into the scheme. The canonization was finally granted in 1457.[11] It was the chapter's most impressive achievement in the 15th century, representing 60 years of sustained effort and consistent planning by a changing group of men. At the same time the popularization of the Use of Salisbury had gone steadily forward. There had been much liturgical advance. The new Ordinal of the 14th century had begun to get out of date; fresh replies were required from the authorities at Salisbury to the *dubia* of perplexed inquirers; provisions were made for the local peculiarities of other dioceses. The *Directorium Sacerdotum* of Clement Maydeston provided a detailed directory, interpreting the general rules of the Ordinal, and illustrating and commenting on the Salisbury rite. The rapid diffusion of the Use is seen in its adoption at St. Paul's cathedral in 1415, where it was introduced by Bishop Richard Clifford, a former canon of Salisbury, and at a steadily increasing number of other cathedral and parish churches, chantries, colleges, and religious houses throughout England, Scotland, Ireland, and Wales. With the introduction of printing, many editions of Salisbury service books were issued. Finally, in 1542, the Convocation of Canterbury ordered all clergy of the province to follow the Salisbury Use.[12]

Other evidence for the chapter's prestige and distinction in the early 15th century is its surprisingly successful, though temporary, resumption of electing its bishop *de gremio* in 1417. Conditions were exceptional, because the election took place in the vacancy of the papacy before the election of Martin V. Eighteen canons, including three dignitaries, were present in person and 23 by proxy, and they chose unanimously by way of inspiration their dean, Master John Chandler, who, although a king's clerk, had been connected with the chapter for the greater part of his life. Archbishop Chichele, himself a former member of the chapter, welcomed the opportunity of recovering the archiepiscopal right of confirming elections; the king agreed, and eventually Martin V gave the papal confirmation.[13] Bishop Chandler's episcopate was a time of active and successful co-operation between bishop and chapter. On his death in 1425 the chapter attempted once more to elect its bishop *de gremio*. This time, however, Martin V obediently provided Robert Neville, the royal nominee, and quashed the election.[14] During the same period the chapter had been able to hold free elections to the deanery also. Its choice of Chandler in 1404 and of Sydenham in 1418[15] had resulted in resident, conscientious, and reforming deans. On Sydenham's provision to Chichester in 1431, however, external influences probably intervened, and Master Thomas Brown, a non-resident canon, who had only been appointed to a Salisbury prebend a few months before the election, in order to qualify him, was chosen.[16] After this few elections seem to have been entirely free.

The chapter continued to be a distinguished body until well after the mid-15th century, and some new enterprises were undertaken, including the building of a new theological lecture room and a library over the west side of the cloister. Four canons were put in charge of this work:[17] Master Gilbert Kymer, the treasurer and future dean, Chancellor of Oxford University, and physician to Henry VI and Humphrey, Duke of Gloucester; Master Nicholas Upton, the precentor, a Wykehamist and author of the *De Studio militari*; Master William Ingram, and Master Thomas Cyrceter, who on his death left many theological and historical manuscripts and sermons to the new library, some apparently in his own handwriting.[18] Shortly

[7] *Canonization of St. Osmund*, ed. A. R. Malden, 236–42.

[8] D. & C. Sar., Reg. Pountney, ff. 50–52.

[9] D. & C. Sar., Reg. Harding, ff. 79*b*, 95; Sar. Reg. Neville, f. 42.

[10] *Canonization of St. Osmund*, ed. A. R. Malden, xxxii, 172–215. [11] Ibid. vi–xxxi, 28 sqq., 167–9, 224–35.

[12] *Use Sar.* ii, xxvi–xxvii, xxx–xxxii.

[13] D. & C. Reg. Pountney, ff. 57, 67–76; Sar. Reg. Chandler, ff. 4–8; *Reg. Chichele* (Cant. & York Soc.), i, 26–40; *Cal. Pat.* 1416–22, 122, 126, 131; *Cal. Pap. Lett.* 1417–31, 81; A. H. Thompson, *Engl. Clergy in later Middle Ages*, 28–29.

[14] D. & C. Sar., Reg. Harding, ff. 66–71, 82–83; Sar. Reg. Neville, ff. 1, 2; *Cal. Pat.* 1422–9, 345; *Acts of P.C.* (Rec. Com.), 1422–9, 269.

[15] D. & C. Sar., Reg. Draper, ff. 74–81; Sar. Reg. Chandler, ff. 13*b*–16.

[16] Sar. Reg. Neville, ff. 10*b*–13*a*; *Fasti Eccl. Sar.* ed. Jones, 218, 316, 413.

[17] D. & C. Sar., Reg. Houchyns, ff. 83, 97.

[18] Cf. *D.N.B.* s.v. Kymer, Gilbert; *Canonization of St. Osmund*, ed. A. R. Malden, xx–xxii; *W.A.M.* li, 492–4; E. M. Thompson and S. M. Lakin, *Cat. Sar. Cath. Libr.* nos. 13, 36, 39, 40, 55, 84, 113, 126, 167, 170, 174.

afterwards the chancellor, Master Andrew Holles, another Wykehamist and former clerk of Archbishop Chichele, came into residence, and in 1454 agreed that theological lectures should be given in the new lecture room at least once a fortnight at his expense.[19] Possibly there was a minor scholastic and artistic renaissance in Salisbury about this time. The mural painting of the Last Judgement on the chancel arch of the chapter's church of St. Thomas, Salisbury, contains an almost life-size picture of St. Osmund, obviously inspired by his recent canonization, and the work suggests that Salisbury artists were in touch with Flemish glaziers.[20] More manuscripts were given to the cathedral library,[21] and the Valley scholars were also active. In 1468 it was suggested that they should be given opportunities of preaching in the cathedral.[22] At the chancellor's grammar school in Exeter Street masters seem always to have been appointed eventually, in spite of occasional difficulties, and by this time were teaching the older choristers and altarists as well as the younger vicars and boys of the city, while the choristers' sub-master in the close apparently taught only the younger choristers.[23] In the 15th century, too, the choristers had a special singing instructor, who was distinct both from their sub-master and from the succentor, and who was frequently the cathedral organist.[24] No additions were made to their property, which was valued at only £35 17*s.* 8*d.*[25] a year in 1535, but they were allowed 13*s.* 4*d.* from the entrance fees of residentiary canons from 1407, and the boy bishop was usually granted the offerings at the high altar on Holy Innocents' Day.[26] An attempt by the masterful precentor, Nicholas Upton, to abolish their free election of their boy bishop was defeated in 1448, though the chapter then passed a statute 'restraining the insolence of the choristers', whose unruly conduct had caused the death of the bishop's vicar choral in a brawl in the close on Holy Innocents' night.[27]

One of the most interesting constitutional changes of the 15th century was made in the organization of the vicars choral. In 1409 they received a formal charter of incorporation from Henry IV, giving them the right to elect their own proctor or head from among themselves as often as and when they pleased; to be called as a body 'The Proctor and Community of the Vicars Choral of Salisbury Cathedral'; to use a common seal; to acquire and hold property in common; to implead and be impleaded, and to prosecute causes. They were, however, still to be appointed by the dean and chapter and obedient to their correction.[28] Perhaps the incorporation did not involve any very startling changes, but the vicars' greater legal independence was shown in royal and episcopal mortmain licences, which allowed the proctor and community of the vicars to acquire an inn and shops in Salisbury valued at £5 a year.[29] Before this such licences had usually been granted to the dean and chapter for the vicars' maintenance, not to the vicars directly. Various other small grants were made to their common fund or common chest.[30] In 1442 they held the rectory of Broad Windsor (Dors.) and by 1535 were drawing 10*s.* annual rent from Orcheston St. George.[31] Their net corporate income as given in the *Valor Ecclesiasticus* amounted to £236 11*s.* 6½*d.* a year.[32] It included £54 17*s.* 6*d.* paid to them as commons by the dean and chapter; £72 13*s.* 4*d.* in stall wages from the individual prebendaries; about £97 from the farms of their churches, and £24 7*s.* in rents.

Important changes in the vicars' daily lives were also made by the institution of a common hall of residence for them in the north walk of the close. The first known reference to it is in 1409.[33] By this time all other English secular cathedrals had colleges or common halls for their vicars.[34] As a result they gradually came to govern themselves in many matters of their daily life, although the dean and chapter always exercised a general supervision. In 1442 an important set of statutes drawn up by the proctor and community of the vicars for the management of their common hall was confirmed by the chapter.[35] These statutes imposed fines for unruly or violent behaviour and language; described the duties of the hall's officers, and made careful provisions for the payment of daily or weekly commons and for entertaining visitors to meals. Not all the vicars were forced to live in hall. The sub-dean and succentor, who were sometimes vicars, were given separate houses annexed to their offices, but the chapter insisted that all vicars of non-resident canons must live there.[36] In addition to the proctor, two senior vicars were appointed annually to be dispensers or supervisors of the common expenses; they drew up a rota of juniors to act as stewards under their direction; the stewards did the catering, but had to be

19 D. & C. Sar., Reg. Houchyns, f. 94; Reg. Burgh, f. 115.

20 A. Hollaender, 'The Doom Painting of St. Thomas of Canterbury, Salisbury', *W.A.M.* l, 351–70.

21 e.g. E. M. Thompson and S. M. Lakin, *Cat. Sar. Cath. Libr.* nos. 32, 75, 143–4, and above, p. 178; cf. N. R. Ker, 'Salisbury Cath. MSS.' *W.A.M.* liii, 153.

22 For de Vaux College see p. 369.

23 Sar. Reg. Chandler, f. 21; Aiscough, ff. 84–85; D. & C. Sar., Reg. Draper, ff. 38–39; Burgh, ff. 18, 31, 124; Machon, f. 33; *W.A.M.* xlviii, 3.

24 *W.A.M.* xlviii, 213, 216.

25 *Valor Eccl.* (Rec. Com.), ii, 85.

26 D. & C. Sar., Reg. Draper, f. 69; Reg. Pountney, f. 2.

27 Ibid. Reg. Burgh, ff. 21–22, 37; *W.A.M.* xlviii, 210–13.

28 *Cal. Pat.* 1408–13, 152.

29 Ibid. 290; Sar. Reg. Hallam, ii, f. 14.

30 D. & C. Sar., Reg. Draper, f. 69; Viring, f. 32; Harding, ff. 41*a*, 95; *Cal. Pat.* 1408–13, 150, 160; *Ceremonies and Processions, Sar.* 268.

31 *Stat. Sar.* 322; *Valor Eccl.* (Rec. Com.), ii, 84.

32 *Valor Eccl.* (Rec. Com.), ii, 84–85.

33 *Stat. Sar.* 55 n.

34 Edwards, *Eng. Secular Cath.* 282–4.

35 *Stat. Sar.* 322–31.

36 D. & C. Sar., Reg. Harding, f. 103*a*.

accompanied by a supervisor whenever they went to buy food in the city.[37] There were also a communar of the vicars, with his office modelled on the chapter's communar, and eight senior vicars, who, with the proctor, presented the community's annual accounts to the chapter for audit.[38] In 1443 the dean and chapter agreed that six senior vicars with the succentor might in future be present at the examination and admission of new vicars by the chapter,[39] when they could presumably raise objections to unsuitable candidates.

Nevertheless, the state of the vicars in the last half of the 15th and in the early 16th century was unsatisfactory. Much can be learnt of their discipline and observance from the episcopal visitations, which were made regularly every seven years from 1394 until at least 1475, when there is a gap in the records. The *detecta* at Bishop Chandler's and Bishop Neville's visitations were mainly concerned with the faults of the vicars.[40] In 1440 and 1447 the records of Bishop Aiscough's visitations suggest a more serious situation.[41] There were complaints about vicars who were frequently absent from choir, were noisy and irreverent when present, neglected their masses, and caused scandals in the close and city by their relations with women. A particularly interesting case was that of John Wallope, who, in addition to quarrelling with his fellow vicars and committing adultery with three women, was accused of heresy at discussions among the vicars in their common hall.[42] This is one of the few surviving references to heresy among the cathedral clergy before the Reformation, but it suggests that debates in the close may have been lively and vigorous. The bishop ordered some deprivations of benefices, a stricter observance of duties, and bible reading at table in the vicars' common hall. The evidence of later visitations and the many cases of delinquent vicars brought before the dean and chapter show, however, that there was no improvement.[43] Moreover, by 1468 the number of vicars at the cathedral had begun to fall. Until then 48 or 49 of the full number of 52 vicars had appeared regularly at visitations, but in 1468 there were only 31.[44] In 1475 Bishop Beauchamp investigated at length the insufficiency in the vicars' numbers. The dean and chapter claimed that suitable persons, especially for the priest vicarages, could not be found, and that such vicars as remained at the cathedral were burdened with too many masses a day.[45] In the 16th century all attempts to maintain the vicars' numbers were abandoned and the canons paid the stall wages of unappointed vicars to the vicars' common fund for the use of the small body which remained.[46]

Other ominous changes in the later 15th century were in the practice of canonical residence. There were normally about ten to twelve residentiaries, including at least two and usually three of the four chief dignitaries, until the end of Gilbert Kymer's deanery in 1463.[47] In the 1440's, however, there were some suggestions of slackness among them. At Bishop Aiscough's first visitation in 1440 some residentiaries were said to go out of town at dawn and return at night of the following day, and still receive their commons for both days. This was forbidden.[48] Then in 1448 the residentiaries, by a temporary ordinance, granted themselves an extra fourteen days' absence for recreation because of the exceptionally bad weather.[49] They were also accused of neglecting their obligations to dispense hospitality.[50] About the same time bishop and chapter agreed that thirteen canonical houses (including the deanery) were to be kept in good repair for residentiary canons, while other houses in the close might be let 'to honourable persons'.[51] This is the first time that the letting of such houses to persons other than cathedral clergy is known to have received official approval, and the decision suggests that the chapter did not expect the number of residentiaries to rise above thirteen in future. In fact it soon began to fall. In 1470–1 there were only nine residentiaries at Salisbury, in 1488 seven, and in 1524 eight. By 1534 only one dignitary, the precentor, was included among the seven residentiaries.[52]

During the same period king and bishop renewed their assaults on the chapter's independence. From the time of Bishop Neville, the chapter still received royal licences to elect its bishops, but had little influence on appointments. A succession of English magnate bishops and civil servants was nominated by the king and provided by the Pope until the eve of the Reformation, when Wolsey and Henry VIII gave the see to Salisbury's only foreign bishop, Lorenzo Campeggio, the papal legate. The chapter continued to elect its dean in general chapters attended at first by large numbers of resident and non-resident canons,[53] but increas-

37 *Stat. Sar.* 326–9.

38 D. & C. Sar., Reg. Harding, f. 104*b*; Burgh, f. 124; Newton, f. 39; *Stat. Sar.* 322.

39 D. & C. Sar., Reg. Houchyns, f. 60.

40 Sar. Reg. Chandler, f. 21; Neville, f. 50; D. & C. Sar., Reg. Pountney, ff. 100–3.

41 Sar. Reg. Aiscough, ff. 83–85, 86–87.

42 Ibid. f. 87.

43 e.g. D. & C. Sar., Reg. Burgh, ff. 97–108; Newton, ff. 5–22; Machon, ff. 172, 178; *Stat. Sar.* 332–7, 323; *Ceremonies and Processions, Sar.* 151–9, 275–6.

44 D. & C. Sar., Reg. Machon, f. 165; cf. Lamb. Reg. Courtenay, f. 149 (1390); Sar. Reg. Neville, f. 49 (1432); Aiscough, ff. 80, 86.

45 *Ceremonies and Processions, Sar.* 157–8.

46 *Valor Eccl.* (Rec. Com.), ii, 85; cf. *Fasti Eccl. Sar.* ed. James, 203–4.

47 D. & C. Sar., Communar's Acct. Rs.

48 Sar. Reg. Aiscough, f. 85.

49 D. & C. Sar. Reg. Burgh, f. 114.

50 Sar. Reg. Neville, f. 50; Aiscough, f. 85.

51 D. & C. Sar., Reg. Houchyns, ff. 104, 113; Sar. Reg. Aiscough, f. 86.

52 D. & C. Sar., Communar's Acct. R. 1470–1, 1488, 1524, 1534.

53 Sar. Reg. Neville, ff. 20*b*–23*a*; Aiscough, ff. 5–10, 17–18, 19 sqq.; Beauchamp, i, ii, ff. 66*b*–70; 143–5; Langton, ii, ff. 7–12; Audley, ff. 166–8.

The Muniment Room, 1834

The Chapter House, 1810

Salisbury Cathedral

ingly pressure was put on it to choose the royal candidate. The bishops regularly attended the elections either by proxy or in person, and in some cases persuaded the chapter to appoint them as compromissaries to nominate the elect. The chapter, worried by this procedure, which usually resulted in the appointment of a non-resident civil servant, began to exact an oath and a bond of £1,000 from all possible nominees that, if elected, they would reside continuously 'as a vicar in his vicarage', or at least pay £100 a year to the residentiaries in compensation.[54] Occasionally it was still able to elect a learned and distinguished resident dean, such as Master Gilbert Kymer, its treasurer, in 1449.[55] On Gilbert's death in 1463 it attempted to exclude Bishop Beauchamp from the election, but was speedily rebuked.[56] The bishop attended the opening of the election, but left early, apparently after ensuring that the Abbot of Sherborne would be chosen as compromissary to nominate Master James Goldwell, a non-resident clerk of Edward IV.[57] In 1473 Bishop Beauchamp himself was able as sole compromissary to nominate John Davyson.[58] In 1486 only 12 canons, 6 resident and 6 non-resident, with 27 proxies of non-residents, were present at the election of another king's clerk, Master Edward Cheyne.[59] In 1502 there was a further fall in attendances. Only five residentiaries were present at the election at which the bishop's proctor simply nominated Master Thomas Ruthall, the king's secretary.[60] The remaining deans of the early 16th century and Reformation period were distinguished men, but non-resident. Several, William Atwater, John Longland, Cuthbert Tunstall, rose to be bishops; several, Longland, Tunstall, Richard Pace, and Peter Vannes, were leaders of the new learning; all enjoyed the royal favour. In other ways also the bishops were attempting to control the chapter more rigorously, though here the chapter had more success in defending its rights. It maintained its right to visit the prebends in the vacancy of the deanery.[61] In 1451 it sent a deputation to Bishop Beauchamp to explain that it adhered to its privilege of not answering him except in chapter.[62] In 1480 a new claim was advanced by Bishop Beauchamp to exercise the sub-dean's archidiaconal jurisdiction in Salisbury city in place of the dean in a vacancy of the sub-deanery. Eventually in the early 16th century the dean's right was acknowledged after an appeal to the king.[63]

More magnificent chantries were also characteristic of the late Middle Ages, as were complaints of an increasing neglect of the founders' ordinances. About nine more chantries or daily masses have been traced to the period before the Reformation,[64] bringing the total to about 33, though probably others have disappeared without any record. Four had special chantry chapels built for them,[65] of which those of Robert, Lord Hungerford, and Bishop Beauchamp, on the outside of the cathedral against the walls of the Lady Chapel, were especially beautiful. All these were more richly endowed than the foundations of earlier centuries. The second Hungerford chapel for Robert, Lord Hungerford, built at a cost of £497, was given ornaments and furniture valued at £250, a house in the close for its two priests, and extensive endowments at Imber, Homanton, in Maddington, and Folke (Dors.).[66] Bishop Beauchamp's chantry, founded in 1481, was for four chaplains, with property valued at £50 a year.[67] The executors of both Dean Kymer in 1475 and of Bishop Beauchamp granted the endowments of their chantries direct to the chantry chaplains instead of to the dean and chapter or some outside college or religious house. This policy was carried a step farther by Bishop Audley, whose executors arranged in 1516 that the chaplain of his chantry should be a body corporate with a common seal capable of defending his right to his property in a court of law.[68] Possibly the founders hoped by these means to prevent a decline in the value of their endowments such as had already taken place in property given for other chantries. The arrangement, however, at least in the case of Bishop Beauchamp's chantry, proved even less satisfactory than the earlier methods. In 1505 one of its chaplains was cited before the bishop to answer for the state of the chantry buildings, which were dilapidated and a scandal.[69] By 1535 the annual value of its property had fallen to £12 10*s.* and there was only one chaplain.[70] Altogether the *Valor Ecclesiasticus* named only ten perpetual chantries served by thirteen chaplains, whose total incomes are estimated at £98 5*s.* 11*d.* a year.[71] Of these, only one, that of Bishop Bridport, had survived from the 13th century; his chaplain was the poorest, with £3 6*s.* 8*d.* a year. Two, the Blunsdon and Clone chantries, had continued from the 14th century, and the remaining seven were 15th- or early 16th-century founda-

54 D. & C. Sar., Reg. Houchyns, f. 99; Burgh, f. 56.

55 D. & C. Sar., Reg. Burgh, ff. 56–66; Sar. Reg. Aiscough, f. 19 sqq.

56 D. & C. Sar., Reg. Newton, ff. 62–63.

57 Ibid. ff. 93–100; Sar. Reg. Beauchamp, I, ii, 66*b*–70.

58 Sar. Reg. Beauchamp, I, ii, 143–5.

59 Sar. Reg. Langton, ii, ff. 7–12.

60 Sar. Reg. Audley, ff. 166–8.

61 D. & C. Sar., Reg. Draper, f. 86; Houchyns, ff. 131–2; Newton, ff. 145–72; Hist. MSS. Com. *1st Rep.* 91.

62 D. & C. Sar., Reg. Burgh, f. 74.

63 Sar. Reg. Beauchamp, II, i, 34–35; D. & C. Sar., Harward's Memorials, ff. 23–30.

64 *Cal. Pat.* 1401–5, 403; 1422–9, 390; 1467–77, 311, 400, 566; 1476–86, 276; *Cal. Fine R.* 1445–52, 143; *L. & P. Hen. VIII*, ii, (1), p. 832; *Ceremonies and Processions, Sar.* 185–6, 210–11, 281–306.

65 Those of Walter, Lord Hungerford, Robert, Lord Hungerford, Bp. Beauchamp, Bp. Audley.

66 *W.A.M.* ii, 93–94; xi, 334–9; xlvii, 458–60.

67 *Cal. Pat.* 1476–85, 276.

68 Ibid. 1467–77, 566; 1476–85, 276; *L. & P. Hen. VIII*, ii, (1), p. 832.

69 Sar. Reg. Audley, f. 127.

70 *Valor Eccl.* (Rec. Com.), ii, 86.

71 Ibid. ii, 86–87.

tions. In addition, allowances were made to the chapter for the maintenance of fifteen daily masses from property belonging to the common or fabric funds, and for the celebration of 62 obits.[72] Possibly the *Valor* is incomplete, or some chantries and obits may have been combined, but even so it seems likely that a number of chantries and obits had disappeared through neglect or failure of their endowments.

The chapter made efforts, particularly in the early 15th century, to increase its fabric fund by buying small pieces of property in and near Salisbury. City property to the value of £5 a year was acquired for the fabric in 1424.[73] This exhausted the chapter's general licence of 1366 to acquire property in mortmain. In 1423 it purchased a further general licence, authorizing it to accept property to the value of another £50 a year for the repair of the tower and spire.[74] The church and manor of Cricklade, given in 1427 partly for Walter, Lord Hungerford's chantry, accounted for most of the property obtained under this licence; the remainder consisted of land and rents to the annual value of 44*s.* in Stratford and Woodford in 1429.[75] The only further common property traced after this was city property purchased for 100 marks in 1467 from a former chapter clerk and Valley scholar, Master William Harding.[76] A few more minor changes took place in the endowments or tenure of the offices and prebends in the period before the Reformation. By 1490 Ebbesborne Wake church had been annexed to the succentor's office,[77] while the three prebends of Upavon, Loders, and Ogbourne, appropriated to Norman abbeys, were transferred by royal orders to the English houses of Ivychurch Priory, Sion Abbey, and the Dean and Chapter of Windsor respectively.[78] The English houses were ordered to pay all customary dues from their prebends, including the stall wages of their vicars choral.

Neither the surviving quarterly account rolls of the communars nor the *Valor Ecclesiasticus* gives a true picture of the income of the canons. The *Valor* gives the first apparently complete list of the chapter's property.[79] In addition to the further property acquired since 1291, it includes lay fees, portions, and pensions from tithes, as well as property outside the diocese, which had been omitted from the *Taxation of Pope Nicholas*. It estimates the annual value of the common fund at £601 12*s.* net or £771 18*s.* 1*d.* gross as against £329 6*s.* 8*d.* in 1291, and of the fabric fund, which was omitted altogether in 1291, at £75 16*s.* 9½*d.* net or £84 16*s.* 9½*d.* gross.[80] Roughly six-sevenths of the common property was derived from the farms of its 21 churches and from tithes; only about one-seventh from lay fees and city property. The total suggests that Salisbury's common fund was fairly rich compared with those of other English secular cathedrals,[81] which ranged from about £275 net or £436 gross a year at Lichfield to £725 net or £773 gross at St. Paul's. No total is given for the value of the dignities and prebends, but it is clear that, although few changes had been made in the extent of the prebends since 1226 or in the dignities since 1291, their assessment had in most cases risen considerably. The treasurership is given as £101 3*s.* as against £86 13*s.* 4*d.*, and the precentorship at £69 6*s.* 8*d.* as against £33 6*s.* 8*d.*[82] Thus the chapter appears to be a much richer body both in its common property and in its separate estates than in 1291. A main difficulty in dealing with the earlier assessments was to know what relation they bore to the canons' actual income. The *Valor* is generally supposed to give the minimum annual rental value of the property,[83] and this is evidently true for Salisbury, for the valuation of sixteen churches appropriated to the common fund is in every case the same or slightly less than the annual farms paid from them by their canon-farmers to the chapter, as given in the communar account rolls for 1534.[84] Thus the *Valor* is the first taxation to give an assessment corresponding to the rental income received by the chapter. These farms, however, had mostly been fixed well before Bishop Mortival's time at a low rate in order to allow a fair profit to the residentiaries who accepted them, and the quarterly communars' account rolls show that they had varied little between 1343 and 1534. Only in a few cases was the ancient farm permanently raised or lowered.

For the greater part of the 14th century the competition for chapter farms among the residentiaries suggests that they were very profitable. The practice of sub-leasing to clerical or lay sub-farmers had, however, apparently become normal by 1402, and the profits from it may have been falling. In that year a change of policy was carried through the chapter by Dean Montagu and Canon Richard Pitts. They asked the chapter to grant seven-year leases to their sub-farmers at Britford and Stourpaine, because sub-farmers who held only annual appointments took all they could from the land and did not trouble to make improvements. The chapter agreed to issue these leases and to allow their renewal for a further seven years

72 *Valor Eccl.* (Rec. Com.), ii, 78–84. About 75 obits had been recorded in the mid-15th-cent. Obit Kalendar: *Stat. Sar.* 3–14.

73 *Cal. Pat.* 1422–9, 234.

74 Ibid. 70; *Acts of P.C.* (Rec. Com.), 1422–9, 37.

75 *Cal. Pat.* 1422–9, 390; 1429–36, 26.

76 *Cal. Close R.* 1461–8, 403; *Ceremonies and Processions, Sar.* 140–2.

77 Sar. Reg. Langton, f. 13.

78 *Rot. Parl.* iv, 179–83 (1422); *Cal. Pat.* 1461–7, 95; *Fasti Eccl. Sar.* ed. Jones, 398, 409.

79 *Valor Eccl.* (Rec. Com.), ii, 72–84.

80 Ibid. ii, 81–82, 84.

81 Cf. ibid. i, 125–8, 298, 360–2; ii, 292–5; iii, 5–6, 135; iv, 8–12; v, 2.

82 The increase in the deanery from £122 to £204 10*s.* is largely due, however, to the inclusion of Heytesbury and Godalming churches.

83 A. Savine, *Eng. Monasteries on Eve of Dissolution*, 73–75; J. Youings, 'Disposal of Devon Monastic Lands', *E.H.R.* lxix, 20.

84 *Valor Eccl.* (Rec. Com.), ii, 78–79; D. & C. Sar., Communar's Acct. R. 1534.

after the end of the first.[85] The frequent general posts in chapter farms among the residentiaries continued throughout the 15th and 16th centuries, but the administration of the estates and collection of tithes were in the hands of sub-farmers with security of tenure for a definite term of years. These sub-farmers were often yeomen or husbandmen of the parishes in which the estates lay, or vicars of the churches from which the tithes were due. In the first three quarters of the 15th century the terms of their leases usually ranged from three to twelve years, though in 1422 and 1447 two leases at least were granted for as long as 22 and 20 years.[86] In a few cases the rents payable are known and are very interesting. When the lease was granted at the instance of a canon-farmer the rent was considerably more than the ancient farm; for example in 1419 the sub-farmer of Kenton and Alvington agreed to pay £133 6*s.* 8*d.* a year or £40 more than the ancient farm, while in 1422 the rent payable from the sub-farmer of Cannings was fixed at £113 6*s.* 8*d.* or £28 more than that due from the canon-farmer.[87] At the same time other farms were leased directly to outside farmers, sometimes, as at Bramshaw in 1404, for the ancient farm, sometimes, as at Homington in 1462, for £2 10*s.* a year less than the ancient farm of £8.[88] Apparently, therefore, the residentiaries were only willing to accept the profitable farms, and when an estate fell into a bad state of repair or was affected by the agricultural depression of the period, it lapsed to the communar, who leased it for whatever he could get. Later, as the number of residentiaries fell, more farms came into the communar's hands. In 1465 it was agreed that dignitaries should be limited to farms worth 80 marks a year according to the old rents, and simple canons to farms worth 40 marks a year.[89] Naturally the farms which included a church were always more popular as canons' options, and their patronage was never leased to sub-farmers.

The chapter's change of economic policy in the early 15th century, and the gradual withdrawal of the canon-farmers from direct administration of their farms, suggests comparisons with parallel changes in the administration of the property of religious houses. There the change was from direct administration to leasing of the demesne or of tithes to outside farmers for terms of years. The reasons were usually a marked decline of income from the property from about 1350; the expenses of administration had to be cut down, and it was found that collecting rents was less expensive than direct cultivation. The agricultural depression may have had the same effect at Salisbury. Details of incomes from chapter farms are not available, but there are general indications that all was not well with the estates. The many suits for dilapidation resulted in very large estimates for repairs; in several cases farms were taken into the communar's hands because they were not fit to be offered to a canon; neglect of the property of the common and fabric funds and of the prebends was alleged at episcopal visitations throughout the 15th century.[90] Moreover, in 1402, when the change of policy was proposed, expenses in promoting the canonization of St. Osmund and for the repair of the fabric were particularly heavy. In 1428 the entrance fee for residentiaries was raised, not only because of these expenses, but also because of 'the decrease in the profits of farms, prebends and other revenues and the tyrannous burdens on the church'.[91] It therefore seems that the policy of leasing the farms for terms of years was, as Dean Montagu's words suggest, a considered attempt to improve them by encouraging the sub-farmers to take more trouble over their administration. The fact that the policy became increasingly popular suggests that it was in time successful. In the early 16th century leases were being granted for much longer terms of 60 and 66 years.[92] The rents charged to sub-farmers rose little, but fines compensated the chapter for the fall in the value of money. In 1539 the cathedral chancellor was said to have been offered a fine of £50 for a lease of Odiham, and in 1541 a £60 fine was received for Folke manor in return for a 60-year lease.[93] In the late 15th and 16th centuries the residentiaries were playing less part in the supervision of their property than they had done in the 14th century. In 1467 the dean and chapter appointed Roger Holles, a citizen of Salisbury, probably a kinsman of their chancellor, Andrew Holles, to be special solicitor of all their business in the royal courts and elsewhere in England for an annual fee of 26*s.* 8*d.* a year.[94] In 1535 a salary of £4 a year was being paid to a John Acton, steward of their lands, a post which in 1536 they offered to Cromwell.[95] The communar, however, continued to be a canon, elected annually from among the residentiaries. In 1516 it was agreed that no residentiary who was also a residentiary at another cathedral could be eligible for election, since the office required the personal presence of its holder all the year round.[96]

THE REFORMATION

The Reformation at Salisbury brought remarkably few constitutional changes. Rather, there was an accentuation of late medieval developments. Most obvious was the extension of the power of the

[85] D. & C. Sar., Reg. Draper, f. 4.

[86] D. & C. Sar., Reg. Harding, f. 24; Burgh, f. 11.

[87] D. & C. Sar., Reg. Harding, ff. 3–4, 24.

[88] D. & C. Sar., Reg. Draper, f. 28; Newton, f. 40.

[89] D. & C. Sar., Reg. Newton, f. 79.

[90] D. & C. Sar. Regs. and Sar. Regs. *passim*; *Ceremonies and Processions, Sar.* 151–3.

[91] D. & C. Sar., Reg. Harding, ff. 79, 95; Sar. Reg. Neville, f. 42.

[92] D. & C. Sar., Reg. Holte and Blacker, ff. 3, 18.

[93] *L. & P. Hen. VIII*, xiv, (1), p. 122; D. & C. Sar., Reg. Holte and Blacker, f. 18.

[94] D. & C. Sar., Reg. Newton, ff. 121–2.

[95] *Valor Eccl.* (Rec. Com.), ii, 82; *L. & P. Hen. VIII*, x, p. 57.

[96] D. & C. Sar., Reg. Houchyns, f. 117.

Crown over both bishop and chapter. Bishops and deans were henceforth nominated by the Crown as a matter of course in letters missive sent to the chapter with its *congé d'élire*; and the deans, like the bishops, were frequently imposed from outside, being apparently no longer required to be members of the chapter before election. Bishop Shaxton and Bishop Capon, like earlier bishops, had to collate to the prebends many nominees of the Crown, of Cromwell, and of other royal officials.[97] An interesting constitutional experiment was that of royal visitations of the cathedral chapters, during which the bishop's jurisdiction at his cathedral was suspended. The system, however, was in full operation only at intervals between 1535 and 1559; since then the Crown has not suspended episcopal authority.[98] The Tudors, moreover, used the royal injunctions issued after their visitations chiefly as a means of carrying through their religious changes. Most of their orders were about images, relics, lights, preaching, theological books to be acquired for the cathedral library, and education. Injunctions on constitutional matters were much more rarely given, and the royal commissioners seem to have found the investigating and interpreting of cathedral statutes a particularly difficult task. The few constitutional changes which they ordered were usually observed only temporarily or not at all, unless they happened ultimately to accord with the development of cathedral customs.[99] It was over 200 years since the last comprehensive revision of the cathedral statutes by Bishop Mortival, and, as at other cathedrals of the Old Foundation, many statutes at Salisbury were at variance with existing custom. Both Mary and Elizabeth I were given power by Parliament to revise cathedral statutes, but little was done. By 1572 a draft was prepared by Archbishop Parker; then the whole project was apparently quashed.[1] The medieval statutes of Salisbury remained in force, and the canons on their admission swore to obey both them and 'the laudable and approved customs' of the church, with the qualification 'in so far as they agree with the Word of God and with the laws of the kingdom'.[2] For the future, when episcopal or archiepiscopal visitors pointed out that the ancient statutes of the church were not observed, or that recent chapter acts were contrary to the statutes, the dean and chapter merely replied that they had sworn to obey the customs as well as the statutes, and that customs were often more in accord than the statutes with the present needs and constitution of their church.[3]

The fall in numbers of resident clergy, already observed in the late 15th century, was confirmed and carried farther, although the residentiary canons remained at about seven or eight throughout the Reformation period.[4] The biggest changes were among the lesser clergy and followed the dissolution of the chantries in 1547–8. The chantry priests disappeared from the cathedral, and the functions and revenues of the vicars choral were much reduced. Masses for the souls of the founders of the chantries were no longer said and the daily High Mass and Mass of the Virgin in the Lady Chapel were also soon to be abolished. The reformers resented the idea that priests should be appointed merely to sing in choir, saying that they were more urgently needed in the parishes, while laymen with good voices could perform the choral duties in the cathedral more efficiently. In 1539 the chapter rejected a lay vicar nominated by Bishop Shaxton for Thomas Cromwell, because he was not a priest and Cromwell's stall in the cathedral was a priest's stall;[5] but by 1547 lay vicars were being appointed, and there was apparently competition for their offices. The vicars choral seem from the first to have had the right of nominating or approving the appointments of lay vicars, and paid their salaries from their common fund. In 1547 fourteen vicars choral agreed at the king's request to the admission of Patrick Forde, layman, as a lay vicar to the next vacant place after the admission of Robert Courtenay, who had already been promised the next vacancy.[6] In 1552 there were still 20 vicars choral, but by 1568 the numbers had fallen to 7 vicars choral and 7 lay vicars.[7] Six vicars choral and 7 lay vicars appeared in 1593, when the sub-treasurer was a lay vicar.[8] His fall in status was doubtless the result of the loss of many of the cathedral treasures, which had reduced the importance of his office. The chief function of the altarists was removed with the destruction of the altars and chantries. Men or boys were still needed to help the vergers to clean the church and to ring the bells (though bell ringing was less frequent than before), but these duties alone were not suitable for former choristers. At first efforts were made to divert some of the revenues from the altarists' stipends to the education of choristers whose voices had broken. Injunctions of Edward VI and Elizabeth I ordered that choristers who had served for five years or more in the church and whose voices had broken should no longer be appointed to do the work of altarists, but should be given an altarist's stipend

97 *L. & P. Hen. VIII*, vi, p. 222; x, pp. 348, 439; xii (2), pp. 256, 266, 446–7, 450; D. & C. Sar., Reg. Holte and Blacker, ff. 179–80.

98 W. H. Frere, *Visitation Articles and Injunctions of Reformation Period*, i, 120 sqq. ii, iii.

99 e.g. the royal injunctions of 1547 and 1559, that the entrance fee for residentiaries should be limited to £20, was observed from 1547 to 1552 but disregarded from 1554: Frere, *Visitation Articles*, ii, 137; D. & C. Sar., Reg. Holte and Blacker, ff. 42, 49, 56, 63–64, 74–75, 134.

1 Frere, *Visitation Articles*, i, 162–5.

2 *Ceremonies and Processions, Sar.* 114.

3 e.g. Hist. MSS. Com. *4th Rep. App.* 128, 131.

4 The highest number found is 8: D. & C. Sar., Harward's Memorials, f. 46; Reg. Holte and Blacker, ff. 21–22; Communar's Acct. R. Apr.–June 1580.

5 *L. & P. Hen. VIII*, xiv (1), p. 240.

6 D. & C. Sar., Reg. Holte and Blacker, f. 43.

7 Hoare, *Mod. Wilts.* Salisbury, 265; D. & C. Sar., Reg. Blacker, ff. 29–30.

8 Sar. Reg. Coldwell, f. 19.

of £3 6*s.* 8*d.* a year for five years to support them while studying at the free grammar school in the close. At the same time three men were to be appointed and paid by the treasurer and two by the Masters of the Fabric to keep the church clean and to ring the bells.[9] For a time these orders were partially observed.[10] By 1593, however, the altarists' portions were no longer given to scholars, but to the lay vicars as a help towards their maintenance.[11] Throughout the greater part of the 17th century and beyond, four or five lay vicars received the traditional payments allotted to altarists in the Middle Ages.[12] The number of choristers also fell. By 1552 they were only 8; in 1569 the chapter declared that they should not exceed 10; in 1580 they were 8; in 1593 6.[13]

The loss and damage to the chapter's property, though serious, was probably less devastating than many of the canons expected. Only six prebends were lost, and five more involved in Bishop Capon's exchanges of property. The prebends of Sherborne, Loders, and Upavon were dissolved with the monasteries which held them; Blewbury prebend, after being appropriated for a time to Wolsey's Oxford college, was annexed to Salisbury bishopric in 1542; while Faringdon and Horton prebends were alienated in Edward VI's reign, Horton going to the Duke of Somerset.[14] In 1542 and 1545 by Acts of Parliament Bedwyn prebend was exchanged for Uffculme (Devon); Charminster and Bere for Ilfracombe (Devon); Axford and Ramsbury for Gillingham (Dors.), which was divided into the two prebends of Gillingham Major and Gillingham Minor; and Ratfyn for Winterbourne Earls.[15] Further losses followed the dissolution of the cathedral chantries, though some of their property was 'concealed' until Elizabeth's reign. The chapter succeeded in retaining the Abbot of Sherborne's canonical house of residence in the close, but lost most of the houses appropriated to chantry chaplains.[16] Pensions payable by religious houses to the chapter were ordered to be paid by the future owners of their lands. With the transfer of the archdeaconry of Dorset to the new diocese of Bristol, the archdeacon ceased to be a member of the chapter. The most disastrous results for later generations were the loss and destruction of many of the cathedral's treasures. In 1539 2 men were employed for 9 days, 4 men for 1 day, and 2 men for a further 15 days on the destruction of St. Osmund's shrine,[17] the long period of demolition suggesting that the jewels were carefully removed. In 1549 the dean and chapter received a royal order to send 2,000 marks' worth of cathedral plate to the king's mint at Bristol.[18] In Elizabeth I's early years there were several further sales of jewels, ornaments, and copes, 'for which there is now no use'. On one occasion at least the buyers were the dean and residentiary canons, only Chancellor Parry protesting at the action and refusing his share of the spoils.[19] The extent of the cathedral's loss can be measured by comparing the rich inventory of jewels, images, vestments, and other treasures made by Master Thomas Robertson, treasurer, in 1536, with an inventory of 1583, which consists of a mere 29 items of little value.[20] Probably much of the medieval stained glass was also removed at this time, for several visitation injunctions of the 1560's and 1570's refer with dismay to the cathedral windows 'broken and open to the rain'.[21]

The most revolutionary changes were naturally in the cathedral services and liturgy. The Use of Salisbury was abolished and the English Prayer Book took its place. In Edward VI's reign and from Elizabeth's reign only two daily services were held at the cathedral in the morning and evening, with a monthly communion, in place of the seven daily canonical hours, the daily High Mass, the daily Mass of the Virgin, and the many chantry masses and obits of the early 16th century. Yet even here there were links with the past, for the first Prayer Book of 1549 was partly compiled from the Use of Salisbury.[22]

Under Bishop Shaxton, Salisbury's first reforming bishop, there was strong Catholic opposition within the chapter, though from the first Cromwell, if not Shaxton, could command some support, and set himself to acquire more. In 1534 Richard Arche, a residentiary canon, wrote to the queen's vice-chamberlain that Dr. Edward Powell and Master John Baker, residentiaries, and others should be discharged as proctors for Salisbury Diocese in the matter of the king's divorce, and the dean and chapter told to elect others named by the king; he himself and Master Thomas Bennet, the bishop's vicar-general, would put Salisbury Diocese on the king's side, but the others were directly against his cause.[23] Powell was speaking, preaching, and writing books against the king's

[9] Frere, *Visitation Articles*, ii, 139; iii, 32–33; *Stat. Sar.* 375.
[10] Cf. Robertson, *Sarum Close*, 130.
[11] Ibid. 144.
[12] e.g. *Stat. Sar.* 380 n.
[13] Hoare, *Mod. Wilts.* Salisbury, 265; *W.A.M.* xlviii, 218–20; Sar. Reg. Coldwell, f. 19.
[14] *Fasti Eccl. Sar.* ed. Jones, 107, 367, 380, 393, 398, 416, 426; *L. & P. Hen. VIII*, iv (2), p. 1865; v, pp. 22, 120, 133, 286; xvi, p. 502.
[15] *Fasti Eccl. Sar.* ed. Jones, s.v. names of prebends; *L. & P. Hen. VIII*, xx (2), p. 411.
[16] e.g. *W.A.M.* xlvii, 385, 387; *Cal. Pat.* 1548–9, 286–7, 426; 1558–60, 308; 1560–3, 555.
[17] *W.A.M.* xlviii, 165.
[18] Hist. MSS. Com. *Var. Coll.* i, 371.
[19] *Fasti Eccl. Sar.* ed. Jones, 236 n.; D. & C. Sar., Reg. Blacker, f. 16.
[20] *Ceremonies and Processions, Sar.* 160–8; *W.A.M.* xliv, 407–10.
[21] Frere, *Visitation Articles*, iii, 367–8.
[22] F. E. Brightman, *The English Rite*, 1915, i, lxxix, 1 sqq.; ii, *passim*; G. Dix, *Shape of the Liturgy*, 613–734, *passim*, especially 645, 659–60. The second Prayer Book of 1552, however, went much farther, altering the structure of the services and following continental rather than English practices and doctrine.
[23] *L. & P. Hen. VIII*, vii, p. 14.

marriage;[24] by 1535 he was a prisoner in the Tower, and was hanged, drawn, and quartered at Smithfield in 1540 for denying the king's supremacy.[25] His canonical house in the close went in 1536 to Thomas Parker, a supporter of Cromwell, who soon succeeded Edward Carne as chancellor.[26] In 1536 too, Master Thomas Bennet gained the precentorship on the death of Richard Dudley, who, as the dean's *locum tenens*, had been resisting Cromwell's claims at the cathedral.[27] Thus three members of the residentiary chapter of seven were now apparently ready to serve Cromwell, and their influence may be seen in its decision of 1536 to offer him the stewardship of its lands.[28] Yet Bishop Shaxton still met with much resistance in his efforts to enforce the royal injunctions. In 1537 Macdowell, the bishop's chaplain, reported that the Pope's name was still in the cathedral missal and the king's orders totally disregarded there. Macdowell's preaching in the cathedral against the Bishop of Rome roused such indignation that deputations against him were sent to the king from the close and city. When he fixed a copy of the king's dispensation for Lent to the cathedral gate it was immediately torn down, and none would search for the culprits. Both he and the bishop were accused of heresy. The resentment aroused by Macdowell, 'an uncharitable and slanderous Scottish friar', is shown by his excommunication by Thomas Bennet, then chancellor of the diocese and in frequent communication with Cromwell.[29] Goodall, the bishop's under-bailiff of Salisbury, complained bitterly of the enormities of the priests in the close and city, who haunted ale-houses and supported relics. The royal injunctions were said to be kept neither by the precentor nor by the subdean, while scholars had even been rebuked for not coming to evensong on a high even.[30] By 1539, however, Goodall wrote to Cromwell that 'the displeasures have accomplished something; now the residentiaries not only preach, but have Bible reading at dinner'.[31]

With the deprivation of Shaxton and the accession of the pliant Bishop Capon most canons seem to have followed their bishop's example in accepting the royal commands. In Edward VI's reign the Italian dean and king's Latin secretary, Peter Vannes, was apparently replaced for a time by an ardent reformer, Thomas Cole, who fled to Frankfort and Geneva in Mary's reign.[32] Mary restored Vannes to the deanery and gave a prebend and house in the close to Thomas Harding, the catholic apologist and future opponent of Bishop Jewel.[33] He and several other canons appointed in Mary's reign were deprived in the opening years of Elizabeth's.[34] On the whole, however, it seems that deprivations for conscience' sake were few at Salisbury. An interesting and perhaps typical figure is Master Thomas Bennet,[35] who first appeared at Salisbury in 1524 as a chaplain of Wolsey, and vicar-general for the absent Bishop Campeggio. Apparently he suffered for a time after Wolsey's fall, being replaced as chancellor of the diocese by Richard Hilley, the cathedral treasurer. But by 1533 he had decided to support Cromwell and the king's divorce, and was soon back in favour. From 1536 he took a leading part in chapter business as precentor, acting frequently as *locum tenens* for the dean. He could occasionally take an independent line with Cromwell. In 1543, with Bishop Capon and other commissionaries, he tried John Marbeck, the Windsor organist, for heresy, and sentenced him to burning, although the sentence was not carried out. Yet Bennet seems to have had no difficulty in continuing to live in the close as precentor in Mary's reign until his death in 1558. Perhaps his chief interest in his later years lay in providing for his many kinsmen and dependants. He had a magnificent monument built for himself in the cathedral before his death, and also took an active interest in the cathedral choristers.[36] Bennet was not apparently alone at Salisbury in adopting a pliant attitude. The famous Vicar of Bray was also a residentiary canon at Salisbury in the reigns of Henry VIII and Edward VI, though he died in 1551, and so the full story of his changes of religion under Henry, Edward, Mary, and Elizabeth cannot be true.[37]

Nevertheless, although the chapter weathered the storm, its moral strength was reduced by the rapid changes. John Jewel, who visited it and other cathedrals of the south-west as royal commissary in 1559 and as archbishop's commissary in 1560, wrote to his friend Peter Martyr in Geneva that 'the cathedral churches have become dens of robbers or more wicked'.[38] Again, on his first visitation as bishop in 1562, Jewel found 'very many things amiss, which we took grievously to heart'.[39] Materially the cathedral was in a deplorable state, with its tower and glass, canonical houses, and close wall approaching ruin. Nature had been taking a hand in the destruction: in 1559 the spire was struck by lightning, and a fissure extended 60 feet downwards from the top. The attitude of the chapter to their bishop may be illustrated by Jewel's remark that 'this happened

24 *L. & P. Hen. VIII*, vii, pp. 14, 279.

25 Ibid. viii, p. 397; *Fasti Eccl. Sar.* ed. Jones, 361 n.

26 *Fasti Eccl. Sar.* ed. Jones, 340; *L. & P. Hen. VIII*, Add. I, i, p. 374.

27 *L. & P. Hen. VIII*, vii, pp. 447, 566; *Fasti Eccl. Sar.* ed. Jones, 332.

28 *L. & P. Hen. VIII*, x, p. 57.

29 Ibid. xii (1), pp. 328, 330–1, 364, 367, 391.

30 Ibid. xii (2), p. 308; xiii (2), p. 235.

31 Ibid. xiv (1), p. 414.

32 *D.N.B.* s.v. Vannes, Peter; Cole, Thomas.

33 Ibid. s.v. Harding, Thomas.

34 *Cal. Pat.* 1558–60, 5, 39, 258.

35 J. M. J. Fletcher, *Thomas Bennet* (1924).

36 See account of school in *V.C.H. Wilts.* v, and D. H. Robertson, *Sarum Close*, 123–6.

37 *W.A.M.* xxi, 165; *Stat. Sar.* 370 n.; D. & C. Sar., Reg. Holte and Blacker, f. 42.

38 G. Burnet, *Hist. of Reformation* (1865), iii, 492.

39 *Stat. Sar.* 396–7.

before I arrived in Salisbury, or it would have been ascribed to my coming'.[40] The spiritual decline and lack of discipline among all ranks of the cathedral clergy seems to have been almost as marked as the material destruction. However, the canons consented to the extension of his visitation for more than the five days allowed by the composition of 1392, and finally thanked the bishop for his work and agreed to the statutes he proposed.[41] These attempted to enforce that all four dignitaries should be continually resident (only one dignitary, the chancellor, was resident in 1562), and provide the customary hospitality and 'feedings' for the lesser cathedral clergy; that the prebendaries should come into residence for a term or pay their fifths for non-residence, and that the individual canons should be responsible for repairing their houses in the close.[42] During the next two years the bishop was several times in chapter examining the cases of canons whom he had pronounced contumacious for not appearing at his visitation. Eventually at least six were deprived of their prebends for simony, infamy, or contempt of the cathedral statutes, while Leonard Bilson, a residentiary, remained in prison for practising magic.[43]

Foremost among the methods adopted by the Elizabethan bishops to improve the state of their chapter was regular visitation. Detailed inquiries were made every seven years; in addition the cathedral was subjected to several metropolitical visitations. At first there was little improvement. Bishop Jewel's second visitation of 1568 revealed serious charges of adultery and incontinence against both canons and vicars as well as much fighting, drinking, and quarrelling among the vicars; some clergy did not attend communion as often as three times a year; the Archdeacon of Wiltshire was said to have two wives; Canon Robert Hooper had been preaching unsound doctrine (though more, it was thought, from inexperience than malice), and Canon John Coleshill was neglecting his duty to dispense hospitality.[44] As time went on the constant episcopal supervision may have had some effect, but progress was very slow. From 1563 the deans, at least, were more frequently resident; several were leading theologians, and their competence is suggested by the fact that until 1604 all were fairly rapidly promoted to bishoprics.[45] But Bishop Jewel's attempt to increase the number of residentiaries and to encourage the prebendaries to come into residence for a short term each year failed completely. An experiment of setting aside Braybrook House in the close as a residential college for the prebendaries ended in a scandal in 1564.[46] The close chapter was now strongly opposed to any increase in the number of residentiaries; and the customary and, later, statutory limitation to seven or six with the dean in the late 16th and early 17th centuries was clearly due to its determination to share the rising profits of residence with as few canons as possible. On the other hand, there was keen competition among the prebendaries for the profitable residentiary places. The bishop kept the right to collate to the residentiary house of Leadenhall, and so to confer one residentiary place; but for the other places royal and magnate influence was sought to put pressure on the close chapter at elections, so that in effect appointments of residentiaries was soon being made by the Crown. By the end of the 16th century a system of pre-election was in full force. In 1585 William Zouch, the precentor, was pre-elected by the close chapter into the fifth vacant residentiary's place next ensuing.[47] Thus dignitaries other than the dean, who attempted to obey the ancient statutes and Bishop Jewel's express order for their continuous residence, would normally for long periods be forced to reside at their own expense without sharing any of the profits of residence and without being admitted to the residentiary chapter or given a canonical house. At the same time the canons' obligations of residence were cut down. Whereas Bishop Mortival's statutes of 1319 had allowed twelve days' absence a quarter to full residentiaries, ordinances of 1571 and 1589 declared that 40 days' residence a quarter would henceforth be sufficient for receiving full commons.[48]

In other ways, however, the bishops achieved some slight success in their efforts to bring the non-resident canons, or, as they were now more usually called, 'prebendaries', into closer connexion with the cathedral. Bishop Jewel insisted that the Pentecostal chapters ordered by the royal injunctions of 1559 should be held annually. All the prebendaries were summoned to these chapters, which continued throughout Whitsun week and gave opportunities for discussion of cathedral business and for grants of taxation from the prebends, particularly for the repair of the fabric. The first was in 1560 when Bishop Jewel attended in person as a prebendary. In 1561, in his absence, no chapter was summoned, but in 1562 he continued his visitation of the cathedral in Whitsun week, requiring the prebendaries to attend.[49] From this time Pentecostal chapters were celebrated fairly regularly during the rest of the 16th century and at intervals in the 17th century up to about 1670. Not all the prebendaries attended, but the custom

40 Ibid. 388, 391, 403; Burnet, *Hist. Reformation*, iii, 500.

41 Frere, *Visitation Articles*, iii, 122–5; *Stat. Sar.* 390–9.

42 *Stat. Sar.* 400–11; Frere, *Visitation Articles*, iii, 126–30.

43 D. & C. Sar., Reg. Blacker, ff. 5–6, 8–11, 14.

44 Ibid. ff. 38–41.

45 *D.N.B.* s.v. Bradbridge, William; Freake, Edmund; Piers, John; Bridges, John.

46 D. & C. Sar., Reg. Holte and Blacker, f. 153; Blacker, ff. 12–14.

47 *Fasti Eccl. Sar.* ed. Jones, 246; D. & C. Sar., Reg. Blacker, pp. 96, 107, 114; Reg. Penruddock, f. 79.

48 D. & C. Sar., Reg. Blacker, f. 58; Reg. Penruddock, f. 12.

49 *Stat. Sar.* 377 380–9, 394, 397 n.

was established, as with the general chapters of the Middle Ages, that absent prebendaries should at least send proxies. A further method of giving the prebendaries some share and responsibility in cathedral work was by preaching turns, requiring every prebendary to preach one sermon a year in the cathedral. The first known rota of preaching turns, drawn up in the reign of Edward VI or Mary, was revised on Bishop Jewel's initiative at the first Pentecostal chapter in 1560,[50] and vigorous efforts were made to enforce it throughout the rest of the 16th and in the 17th centuries. The arrangement that absent prebendaries might pay a deputy to preach their sermons had, however, to be accepted.

Henceforth the cathedral clergy were officially encouraged to have more contacts with the diocese and city. The canons were more insistently required to provide sermons and hospitality at the churches belonging to their prebends and common fund, as well as at the cathedral,[51] where greater emphasis on preaching took the place of the chancellor's theological lectures, and the lecturer disappeared.[52] High fixed seats were erected in the body of the church for the mayor and corporation, who now attended the Sunday services and sermons with their wives.[53] These cumbersome seats caused many disputes about precedence, in which the wives of the cathedral clergy were also involved, and in 1634 Archbishop Laud ordered their removal; for the future only movable seats were to be used.[54] Social changes were taking place in the close, for which the canons' wives were largely responsible. Elizabeth I had at first disapproved of wives of the clergy living in the cathedral close, but had been unable to prevent it. By James I's reign they had an established position, and Dean Gordon's French wife, Dame Geneviève, who was both intelligent and determined, emerged as a dominant figure. Her letters to Secretary Nicholas throw interesting light on life in the close.[55] Salisbury became a centre of fashion when the Stuart kings came to stay with their courts, lodging in the close.[56]

A few signs of a gradual revival in cathedral life may be noticed. There was a big improvement in the cathedral fabric. Much money was spent on it in the late 16th and early 17th centuries, so that by 1634 it could be said: 'no fault is found with the fabric save the pavement and cloisters and some other small defects'.[57] The Gorges memorial, built in the cathedral about this time to commemorate Sir Thomas Gorges and his Swedish wife, suggests a revival of interest in art. The muniments which, on Bishop Jewel's accession, were in a state of decay and complete disorder, were in 1607 and 1634 kept duly under lock and key and were claimed to be safe at least from vermin and bad weather.[58] There is less evidence for interest in the library. It apparently had few manuscripts of sufficient interest to tempt collectors like Archbishop Parker or Sir Robert Cotton. Bishop Jewel was able to send only one book in Old English to Parker, saying he had 'ransacked our poore library to find it'.[59] Bishop Guest gave many printed books and Dean Gordon in the early 17th century also left books;[60] but the dean and chapter were careless custodians. A number of their more interesting medieval manuscripts found their way to Oxford at this time.[61] There were some learned canons and prebendaries. Dean Gordon was a theologian, a scholar of Greek, Hebrew, and oriental languages, and a writer in verse and prose; two prebendaries, Richard Hooker, author of the *Ecclesiastical Polity*, who died in 1600, and Thomas Fuller, the church historian, a prebendary from 1631, made outstanding contributions to the thought and history of the English Church; William Camden, author of the *Britannia*, was a prebendary from 1589 to 1624.[62] Some able masters were appointed to the cathedral grammar school, which had been refounded in the close by about 1540, apparently mainly for the choristers' benefit.[63] The boys, however, apparently suffered increasing ill treatment and neglect in their common house under their sub-master.[64] Their revenues fell in value; about 1620 they ceased to live in common; in 1629 their numbers were permanently limited to six, and the chapter decided that for the future they should be paid salaries of £4 or £3 a year each to support themselves.[65] When the Stuart kings visited the city additional choristers had to be brought from Windsor to augment the choir.[66] This neglect of the cathedral choristers is surprising, because there was a genuine love of church music in Salisbury at this time, and much interest in its development. The cathedral had some fine composers and musicians among its organists and lay vicars, including the tempestuous John Farrant who attempted to murder Dean Bridges in his study, and, on failing to do so, returned to finish singing the anthem in choir, and the Lawes family in the early 17th century.[67] The Puritans condemned their music

50 *Stat. Sar.* 386, 514–15.
51 Hist. MSS. Com. *4th Rep.* i, *App.* 128–9.
52 Ibid. 131.
53 Ibid. 130; Hoare, *Mod. Wilts.* Salisbury, 320–1, 339, 385.
54 Hist. MSS. Com. *4th Rep.* i, *App.* 130.
55 *Cal. S.P. Dom. Add.* 1580–1625, 612.
56 e.g. *Cal. S.P. Dom.* 1637–8, 524; Robertson, *Sarum Close*, 160–2.
57 Hist. MSS. Com. *4th Rep.* i, *App.* 129.
58 Ibid. 130; C. R. Everett, 'Episcopal Visitation of Salisbury, 1607', *W.A.M.* l, 175, 180.
59 *W.A.M.* liii, 153, 156.
60 *Stat. Sar.* 372 n.; Hist. MSS. Com. *6th Rep. App.* 683–4.
61 *W.A.M.* liii, 156–62.
62 *Fasti Eccl. Sar.* ed. Jones, 392, 397, 405, 407, 411; Hist. MSS. Com. *6th Rep. App.* 683–4; *D.N.B.*
63 For the moves and history of the school see *V.C.H. Wilts.* v.
64 For the choristers' school in 1634 see Hist. MSS. Com. *4th Rep.* i, *App.*, 129–30.
65 Robertson, *Sarum Close*, 127–80; *W.A.M.* xlviii, 214–15.
66 Robertson, op. cit. 161.
67 Ibid. 123, 146–58, 167, 169–71.

for being too formal and curious, but George Herbert, poet and parish priest of Bemerton, loved it and found inspiration in his visits to the cathedral in the early 1630's.[68]

Such contrasts are typical of the growing diversity in cathedral life under the early Stuarts, when there was both piety, learning, and striving for order and discipline, along with lack of restraint, negligence, and worldliness. At the same time there were the complications of the widely differing religious views. The citizens of Salisbury were largely Puritan; the bishops conciliatory to them; the deans increasingly inclined to the High Church party, while among the canons were colourful and clashing personalities, some unattractive, a few devout and efficient.

A change from the attitude to church ceremonies of the Elizabethan clergy possibly began in Dean Gordon's time. Although a Scot who had been in the service of Protestant leaders in France, he came so far from his earlier views when preaching before James I in 1605 as to vindicate the use of cross, cap, and surplice.[69] In 1607 the order of 1604 for wearing surplices and hoods was thought to be observed at Salisbury, though the canons agreed that copes were not yet worn at communion.[70] The medieval copes had long since been sold or used up as pulpit cloths or cushions, while the ancient payments of cope money by the canons had been diverted to the fabric fund.[71] About the same time large sums were spent on enlarging and repairing the organ.[72] Some gifts of plate and ornaments were made to the cathedral treasury; the inventory of 1624–5 shows that it was then far more adequately supplied with plate than in 1583 or 1601.[73] The cathedral bells were repaired.[74] In Bishop Davenant's time the different points of view within the church became apparent. The deans in particular asserted their independence of the bishop and took the opposite side in constitutional and religious controversies in cathedral and city. These differences suggest that even after the Reformation Salisbury dean and chapter had retained greater independence of their bishop than other English chapters. Dean Bowle strenuously opposed the bishop's claim to sit in chapter and take part in the election of a music teacher of the choristers.[75] The result was a disputed election, the bishop and three canons voting for John Holmes, son of the former master, the dean and the three other canons for Giles Tompkins, organist of King's College, Cambridge. Appeals to the archbishop and king followed. Eventually the king decided in favour of the dean's party, though its victory was made to appear less decisive by the appointment of Tompkins by the king 'by way of provision'.[76] Dean Mason, Dean Bowle's successor, and tutor to Prince Charles, was an open supporter of Laud against the bishop. Their views clashed in 1633 over the public submission of Henry Sherfield, Recorder of Salisbury, for destroying a stained glass window in St. Edmund's Church. Dean Mason and Laud were victorious, achieving a full public submission.[77]

In another quarrel about this time, over the admission by royal letters of Dr. Humphrey Henchman, the precentor, as a supernumerary residentiary at the cathedral, Dean Mason and Bishop Davenant were, however, united against a majority of the chapter. This quarrel throws light on the divisions, personalities, and motives within the chapter. Henchman was a kinsman of Bishop Williams of Lincoln,[78] who had spent one year as Dean of Salisbury in 1620–1 while waiting to be transferred to the deanery of Westminster. From there his promotion was rapid, but he continued to exercise a strong influence over Salisbury chapter in opposition to the rising influence of Laud. By 1633 it was claimed that Bishop Davenant, Edward Thornburgh, a residentiary canon, and Henchman, the precentor, all owed their appointments to him, while he could on occasion command the vote in chapter of Canon Giles Thornburgh, an elder kinsman of Edward.[79] The bishops of Lincoln and Salisbury were said to 'drive in one yoke', and it seemed to Dr. Matthew Nicholas, a younger brother of Secretary Nicholas and a pre-elected residentiary, that the best way of preventing Henchman from being admitted as a residentiary before him was to play on Dean Mason's fears that Laud, then Bishop of London, would be angry with him for doing so much for a kinsman of the Bishop of Lincoln.[80] The dean, however, was not intimidated, while Bishop Davenant maintained that the Bishop of London was intelligent and would understand the situation at Salisbury. Henchman was a 'true resident' and of greater service to the church than any of the other canons. He had been precentor for ten years; had performed all the duties of the office, including those of residence and hospitality, without ever being admitted as a residentiary or receiving any profits of residence.[81] The attitude of the rest of the chapter seems to have been dictated partly by their anxiety not to offend powerful outside influences, partly by their desire not to share the profits of residence among eight instead of seven residentiaries.[82] By appealing to these last motives

68 I. Walton, *Life of George Herbert*, 1670, p. 60.

69 *D.N.B.*; *Cal. S.P. Dom.* 1603–10, 213.

70 *W.A.M.* l, 175, 181.

71 Hist. MSS. Com. *4th Rep.* i, *App.* 130.

72 *W.A.M.* xlviii, 222–3; Hist. MSS. Com. *Var. Coll.* i, 353.

73 *W.A.M.* xxxix, 30–36; xliv, 407–9.

74 *W.A.M.* l, 182.

75 *Cal. S.P. Dom. Add.* 1625–49, 364.

76 Ibid. 1628–9, 586, 593; 1629–31, 13, 17, 138; D. & C. Sar., Shuter's Memorials, ff. 100–2.

77 *Cal. S.P. Dom.* 1631–3, 267, 538–9, 571–2; 1633–4, 8, 19, 21, 351. See also above, p. 37.

78 Ibid. 1633–4, 65. For Williams and Henchman see *D.N.B.*

79 *Cal. S.P. Dom.* 1633–4, 122, 151.

80 Ibid. 122, 144–5, 151, 162, 227.

81 Ibid. 77–78, 400–1.

82 Ibid. 65, 151, 156, 181, 198–9, 214, 241, 246, 249, 306.

the two pre-elected residentiaries, Dr. Matthew Nicholas and Dr. Thomas Mason, whose claims to residentiary places were prejudiced by Henchman's admission, detached the two Thornburghs from their allegiance to Bishop Williams, and persuaded them with two other residentiaries to petition the king and Laud for the repeal of the royal letters.[83] However, their opposition was not very convincing, especially as they had already accepted Henchman's large entrance fee for residence and divided it up among themselves.[84] Early in 1634 the king on Laud's advice ruled that Henchman was to continue as a supernumerary residentiary, but with single commons like the other residentiaries, not with the double commons anciently due to dignitaries. Thomas Mason and Matthew Nicholas were to have the next two vacant residentiary places. After this the next vacant residentiary place was not to be filled, and the number of residentiaries was to be permanently reduced to six with the dean. There were to be no more pre-elections, and dignitaries were to be as capable as others of being chosen as residentiaries.[85] From this time until the Cathedrals Act of 1840 the number of residentiaries remained fixed by royal ordinance at six with the dean, and the dignitaries permanently lost their claim to double commons.

In the same year Archbishop Laud's visitation of the cathedral revealed a complete lack of system and some scandals in the practice of residence. The canons confessed that they did not know what the times of their residence should be. 'We do not dispense each other, but everyone keeps residence at his own discretion and yet receives all profits as if continually resident.' They thought that sometimes all the residentiaries were absent from the services, but never all absent from their houses, and that all were not absent from the church for many weeks together. Only old Canon Barnston, Canon Henchman, and, before he was called away on royal service, Dean Mason, were not severely criticized for their church attendances and only these three were said to be laudable in hospitality. By others neglect of hospitality was freely admitted. Canon Lee declared that he was too poor to be hospitable, and informed the archbishop's commissary that other canons were very sparing in hospitality. Edward Thornburgh was further accused by Lee of flying into violent passions as a result of intemperate eating and drinking, and Osborne of using bad language. The most serious charge was brought against Canon Seward by Henchman and Lee. He was said to have separated a kinswoman from her husband, to have had the husband put in prison, and to be keeping her at his house in the close in the greatest luxury. Lee himself presented a long and rambling account of his claims to precedence and of his grievances.[86] The reasons for Bishop Davenant's and Dean Mason's insistence on the admission of Henchman as a supernumerary member of such a chapter are self-evident, especially since the dean was likely to be absent for long periods. As a result of the visitation a new statute for residence, according to the canons of the Church of England of 1604, was drawn up by the chapter and confirmed by the king. In future two canons were to be required to keep residence and open house in the close in each quarter of the year, and to be present daily at morning and evening prayers; on 60 of the 90 days their personal attendance at the services was necessary under pain of a 5*s.* fine for every absence; on the remaining 30 days a substitute was allowed, so long as he was a residentiary canon. A rota of residence was drawn up accordingly.[87] Thus a three-monthly residence, similar in some ways to the plan of Richard Poore in the early 13th century, was finally accepted under outside pressure and probably for the first time by the whole residentiary chapter at Salisbury, though this now consisted of only seven or eight canons in place of the 52 for whom Poore had legislated. The gradual abandonment by the residentiaries of the 16th and 17th centuries of the long annual residence customary in the 14th and 15th centuries was not due solely to their laziness and neglect of duty. It was also a necessary result of the orders of the post-Reformation church for their personal residence and hospitality at their prebendal and other churches in the diocese for most of the year. The canons of the Church of England of 1604 specifically required this, allowing to cathedral canons only three months' absence at their cathedral; and Archbishop Laud made searching inquiries at his visitation about its observance.[88] Though most of the canons had been remiss in this as in their other duties, Barnston and Henchman at least were said to have been assiduous in preaching and hospitality at their churches in the diocese.[89] The statute of 1635 now regulated the position at the cathedral, where changes obviously had to be made if the rules for the churches of the prebends and the common fund were to be observed. Much of the disorder in the cathedral in the years before 1635 was probably due to each canon making his own rules to meet conditions for which the ancient statutes did not provide. After 1635 discipline seems to have been tightened up. The new dean was Dr. Richard Baylie, husband of a niece of Archbishop Laud, Vice-Chancellor of Oxford University and President of St. John's College. He spent much of his time in Oxford, but dispensed lavish hospitality 'like a cardinal' on his visits to Salisbury.[90] In his absence the real power in the close lay with Henchman. Matthew

83 *Cal. S.P. Dom.* 1633–4, 198–9, 241, 246, 306.
84 Ibid. 400; D. & C. Sar., Shuter's Memorials, ff. 135–6.
85 *Cal. S.P. Dom.* 1633–4, 455–6.
86 Hist. MSS. Com. *4th Rep.* i, *App.* 128–35.
87 *Stat. Sar.* 412–19.
88 Hist. MSS. Com. *4th Rep.* i, *App.* 127–9.
89 Ibid. 128, 130, 135.
90 *D.N.B.*; *Cal. S.P. Dom.* 1639–40, 606.

Nicholas, who was admitted as a residentiary in 1637, wrote in the following year, 'The order about residence has long been put into execution. Two residents are present in each quarter and attend constantly at the services. . . . Dr. Henchman is now the only visible man in our church.'[91]

The history of the vicars choral in the 40 years preceding the outbreak of the Civil War faithfully reflects the history of their masters, the residentiary canons. The visitations of 1607 and 1634 reveal many examples of negligence and disorder among the choral and lay vicars, as among the canons. They were irregular in their attendances at the church services. The choir was noisy because the vergers did not stop the laity from tramping up and down and talking in the church in service time, and the vicars broke the rule about talking in choir. Some complaints were made about the vicars' singing. In addition the canons maintained in 1607 that there were a few drunkards, haunters of taverns, and sowers of dissension among them. The vicars, like the choristers, ceased to live a common life in their hall of residence about 1620.[92] This was a natural development, now that most vicars were married. More serious were the dissensions which arose between the choral and lay vicars. The small corporation of six vicars choral opposed any increase in its own numbers and any proposals for sharing its increased revenues with the lay vicars. While poverty had been a main reason for the rapid fall in the vicars' numbers in the late 15th and 16th centuries, the further limitation of their numbers in the early 17th century was due, as with the canons' numbers, to the desire of the small established body to keep the profits of their steadily rising revenues for themselves. As a result, the cathedral had much difficulty in attracting good basses and counter tenors to serve as lay vicars. In 1604 the brilliant Thomas Lawes resigned because of his small salary.[93] This caused the chapter to intervene. In 1605 it insisted that the vicars choral must pay £12 a year each to lay vicars with bass voices instead of the normal £8 13*s.* 4*d.* and that for the future at least three and if possible four laymen were to be basses or counter tenors. As a concession to the vicars choral, however, it agreed that the lay vicars might temporarily be reduced from eight to seven, so that the eighth layman's salary might be divided between the two basses.[94] Thomas Lawes was then readmitted as a lay vicar without loss of seniority, but the struggle of the lay vicars against the vicars choral continued and eventually came before the bishop and archbishop. The trouble lay largely in the choral vicars' administration of their property. The value of their lands was increasing, but they refused to raise the old medieval rents, preferring to charge large fines for the renewal of leases, which they at once shared out amongst themselves. Thus their regular annual income remained roughly the same as in 1535, and they declared that this alone could be drawn upon for payment of the lay vicars' stipends, as well as for their own commons and dividends. Shortly before 1615 the archbishop inhibited them from renewing any more leases until an order had been made.[95] In 1624 an agreement was drawn up by which the vicars choral promised not to renew any more leases until they had completely run out. Then the property was to be leased for one, two, or three lives at improved rents. Two-thirds of the increased rents were to go to the vicars choral and one-third to the lay vicars. In return the chapter agreed that the lay vicars should remain at seven until an eighth layman could be paid a sufficient stipend out of the increases; that all fines for renewal of leases should still belong to the vicars choral only; and that the lay vicars' stipends should not exceed £20 a year.[96] By 1644 a new lease of Laverstock rectory for three lives raised the annual rent from £15 to about £85, which according to the Parliamentary Survey of 1649 was about £130 a year less than its actual value, and the lay vicars pressed for increased stipends.[97] After the Restoration all seven received £20 a year but the eighth was never reappointed.

A similar state of affairs prevailed on the chapter's estates. Here there was no further loss of property, save the annexation of Shipton prebend to the Regius Chair of Civil Law at Oxford by Act of Parliament in 1617.[98] But in the late 16th and early 17th centuries there was a steady rise in the value of the property, and, like the vicars, the canons normally refused to lease their lands at rents corresponding to the improved value. The changed situation can best be seen in the Parliamentary Survey of the chapter's lands made in 1649–50, which gives not only the reserved rents of the lands and churches and their assessment for taxation, but also the actual value. For 40 prebends the total assessment for taxation was only £1,400 6*s.* 8*d.* a year and in all cases corresponded to the assessment in the *Valor Ecclesiasticus.* The reserved rents were usually the same or very slightly higher than the taxation value. But the gross annual value was often eight to ten times as great. Thus the gross value of the small prebend of Alton Australis had risen to about £197 a year, although the annual rent paid by its farmer was only £20, and its taxation £19 10*s.* The gross value of the 'golden' prebend of Teignton Regis was about £654, its rent £74 6*s.* 8*d.*, and its taxation £63 13*s.* 4*d.* In the case of the dignitaries' estates the reserved rents paid to the chancellor and treasurer had been raised from £56 and £101 in 1535 to £86 and £174 respectively, while

[91] Ibid. 1637–8, 524; 1637, 112.

[92] *W.A.M.* l, 179–84; Hist. MSS. Com. *4th Rep.* i, *App.* 129–35.

[93] Robertson, *Sarum Close,* 169.

[94] D. & C. Sar., Reg. Mortimer, ff. 160–1.

[95] Sar. Dioc. Regy., Vicars Choral Box, I. Vanderplank's Book, ff. 37–38.

[96] Ibid. ff. 25–32.

[97] Bodl. Rawlinson MS. C. 421, f. 33; E. J. Bodington, 'Church Survey, Wilts. 1649–50', *W.A.M.* xl, 403.

[98] *Fasti Eccl. Sar.* ed. Jones, 416.

their gross values were given as £559 and £1,197.[99] The position on the estates of the deanery, precentorship, and common fund was similar. The commissioners frequently remarked that a church or estate was worth £75, £130, or, in the case of Bishop's Cannings, as much as £681 a year more than the annual rent paid by the farmer.[1] This was due to the increasingly large fines for renewal of leases, some of which, amounting to over £1,000, can be traced in the chapter lease books which are extant from 1608. In spite of the royal injunctions that leases should not be granted for more than 21 years, most of the larger estates and churches were now leased for three lives. In addition to the fines the residentiaries also had the patronage of the churches belonging to the common fund. These advowsons now passed to each residentiary in order of seniority,[2] and were occasionally sold by them, though the sale of the advowson of Britford church for £70 by Canon Edward Thornburgh in 1634 raised such an outcry against simony that it had to be cancelled before payment was made.[3]

THE CIVIL WAR

The period of the Civil War and the Commonwealth saw the only complete break in the chapter's history, when the whole institutional structure and anglican form of worship was swept away and a new Presbyterian system established in its place at the cathedral. It is difficult to discover how long the chapter continued to function. The abolition of deans, chapters, vicars choral, and choristers was made law in 1648, and was followed in 1649 by the Act for the Sale of Deans' and Chapters' Lands.[4] Many individual canons and prebendaries, however, were ejected long before this under the parliamentary order of 1643 which required the sequestration of the property and benefices of all those who had helped to raise arms against Parliament. No entries were made in the chapter act books between 28 November 1642 and 13 September 1660, but the fabric accounts continued into 1643 and included payments to workmen for taking down the organ. The clerk of the works also paid money to the watch at the close gate and to a watch at the church porch during the early fighting in Salisbury.[5] Records of the dean's court are extant as late as 1645,[6] and new prebendaries were appointed in the place of those who had died in 1643, 1644, and 1645, though they were reinstalled in 1660 to safeguard them from charges that their appointments were illegal.[7] As early as 1641 a puritan, John Strickland, later a member of the Westminster Assembly, was elected as minister by the vestry of the chapter's church of St. Edmund, Salisbury, although in his absence in London Thomas Mason, a residentiary canon, apparently officiated, preached against Parliament, and publicly prayed for the success of the royalist forces. Mason seems to have remained in charge at the cathedral for some years. When the parliamentary forces were in Salisbury, probably in 1644–5, he was said never to have preached, but to have kept the church shut. In July 1646 he was accused before the County Committee of Wiltshire of receiving rents due to the dean and chapter, disposing of them as he pleased, and of sending £20 to Dean Bailey in Oxford. He denied on oath that he had the chapter rent-roll, but, when pressed, produced it the next day. He refused to take the Covenant, saying he would stand for the Prayer Book while he lived.[8] After 1646 there is little evidence that the chapter had any authority at the cathedral or in its city churches, though Canon Matthew Nicholas, most of the choral and lay vicars, the schoolmaster, and two vergers were apparently in possession of their houses in the close in 1649–50 when the Parliamentary Survey of the close was made.[9] In 1646 another puritan member of the Westminster Assembly, Dr. John Conant, whom the chapter had refused in 1642, was appointed to its church of St. Thomas, Salisbury; a third, Stanley Gower, to its church of St. Martin, Salisbury, in 1648; and in July 1648 Dr. Faithful Tate became Presbyterian minister at the cathedral with a salary of £150 a year and Canon Mason's house of Leadenhall in the close for his residence.[10] In 1649 it was declared that he 'preacheth twice in the cathedral every Lord's Day, and alone supplieth the ministeriall office there'. It was presented as convenient that 'Our Ladye church be made a parish churche'.[11] Soon after the Survey the city corporation decided to buy four canonical houses in the close for £800 as permanent residences for the four Presbyterian ministers of the city, in the hope that the purchase money would eventually be raised by the parishioners.[12] Other sales of the chapter's property within and outside the close were made. The city magistrates assumed authority over the close, and in 1656 Cromwell's charter to the mayor and corporation gave them full rights of jurisdiction over the former liberty of the close

[99] Sar. Dioc. Regy., Wm. Wastfield's Collection: 'A Perfect Survey of the Bishopric' (unfoliated); apparently a contemporary copy of the parliamentary survey. It always gives the gross and not the net annual values.

[1] *W.A.M.* xl, 253–72, 297–317, 392–416; xli, 1–39, 105–28, *passim*.

[2] Cf. *Stat. Sar.* 364–7.

[3] *Cal. S.P. Dom.* 1633–4, 505; Hist. MSS. Com. *4th Rep.* i, *App.* 129.

[4] W. A. Shaw, *Hist. Eng. Church*, 1640–60 (1900), i, 120–1; ii, 213–14.

[5] Robertson, *Sarum Close*, 194.

[6] Sar. Dioc. Regy., Act Bks. of Dean's Court.

[7] *Fasti Eccl. Sar.* ed. Jones, 403, 411, 429, 431.

[8] J. M. J. Fletcher, *Incumbents of Salisbury Churches during the Commonwealth*, 14–16; A. G. Matthews, *Walker Revised*, 377.

[9] A. R. Malden, 'Survey of the Close in 1649', *Trans. Sar. Field Club*, i, 133, 167–71; ii, 81–87.

[10] Fletcher, op. cit. 1–8, 17; *Trans. Sar. Field Club*, i, 97–98.

[11] *W.A.M.* xl, 396.

[12] Hoare, *Mod. Wilts.* Salisbury, 415–16; Fletcher, *Incumbents of Salisbury Churches*, 15–16.

with the patronage of the dean and chapter's hospital of St. Nicholas by Harnham Bridge which they had long coveted.[13]

The Presbyterian system probably did not take very firm root at Salisbury, particularly at the cathedral and in the close. Faithful Tate had left Salisbury by 1650. The only successor to him who has been traced was a T. Rashleigh, minister at the cathedral about 1658–9.[14]

The cathedral itself seems to have suffered less damage than almost any other cathedral in the country. In 1644 it was plundered by a parliamentary force, and its plate and vestments sent to London to be shown before the House of Commons, but the plate was soon restored.[15] The destruction of the images on the west front of the cathedral and of what remained of the medieval stained glass has sometimes been attributed to this period, but the images and much of the glass were more probably destroyed in Edward VI's reign, while Wyatt in the 18th century was probably responsible for the removal of most of the remaining glass.[16] The heaviest fighting in the city was in 1644–5, when the parliamentary leader, Ludlow, entrenched himself in the close and was attacked there by a royalist force. He had to retire on Harnham, leaving his prisoners and a small body to defend the belfry. The royalists then set fire to the door of the belfry and smoked the defenders out. Further damage was done later by Dutch prisoners in the cloisters. In 1653 the Mayor of Salisbury wrote to the government asking for their removal; he said they had already done much damage to the cloister pillars and to the windows of the library.[17] Evidently the city authorities, having assumed jurisdiction over the cathedral, were now anxious to protect it. The cathedral apparently owed its remarkable preservation throughout the period largely to the generosity and loyalty of local gentry, possibly members of the Hyde family, who secretly employed workmen to keep it in repair. Walter Pope, the friend and biographer of Bishop Seth Ward, tells the story of how, when asked who paid them, the workmen answered, 'They who employ us will pay us; trouble not yourselves to inquire who they are; whosoever they be, they desire not to have their names known.'[18] The bishop's palace, however, and the canonical houses suffered greater damage and dilapidations than the cathedral.

A few glimpses may be caught of the doings of some of the ejected cathedral clergy during these years. The bishop, Brian Duppa, Prince Charles's tutor, stayed with Charles I during his imprisonment, and afterwards lived in retirement at Richmond (Surr.), where he continued to baptize children according to the rites of the Church of England. Of the residentiary canons, four died;[19] and the remaining three, Dean Bailey, Humphrey Henchman, and Matthew Nicholas, all seem to have joined the royal army and had their estates and benefices sequestrated. Later, on the surrender of the royalist garrisons, they were able to enjoy the advantages of compounding for their private estates at the low fine of a tenth without taking the oath to the Covenant, though Matthew Nicholas refused to do this until the king's execution. Henchman was apparently treated generously by the Dorset Committee for Compounding, which in April 1648 forbade any further sequestration of his real estate and allowed him to have its profits since 1646. By 1649 he was again living in the close at Salisbury, though not in his canonical house. In 1651 he helped Prince Charles to escape after the battle of Worcester.[20] Of the prebendaries, many also joined the royalist armies and were taken prisoner at the surrender of the garrisons at Oxford, Dartmouth, and Arundel. Some of the richer ones then compounded for their private estates, while the wives of the others were usually granted fifths from the incomes of their former benefices. Many wives undoubtedly suffered; others showed that they could look after themselves. After their ejections the prebendaries took different ways. Two, Richard Steward, Dean of St. Paul's and prebendary of Alton Borealis, and John Earle, Chancellor of Salisbury, joined the exiles in Paris.[21] Some settled down in country retreats or at Salisbury, but continued secretly to correspond with members of the royalist party or to use the Prayer Book. Others wholly or partially conformed and so managed to keep one of their livings. Thomas Fuller, the historian, after years of deprivation, submitted to seeking the approval of Cromwell's Board of Triers and gained admission to a living in Middlesex. Some found opportunities for study and produced notable books, but those without private means had a hard struggle to exist. John Gregory, the historian of the boy-bishops at Salisbury, whom Wood called 'the miracle of his age for critical and curious learning', died in poverty and obscurity near Oxford.[22] Nothing is known of the cathedral choristers throughout the period, although their grammar master continued to teach in the close. Several

13 Hoare, *Mod. Wilts.* Salisbury, 437–8; *Cal. S.P. Dom.* 1655–6, 330.

14 Fletcher, *Incumbents of Salisbury Churches*, 18; C. Wordsworth, 'Wilts. Ministers, 1643–62', *W.A.M.* xxxiv, 185; W. A. Shaw, *Hist. Engl. Church*, ii, 597.

15 *Cal. S.P. Dom.* 1644, 408; Hoare, *Mod. Wilts.* Salisbury, 397.

16 *W.A.M.* iii, 119–23.

17 Hoare, *Mod. Wilts.* Salisbury, 397–400; *Cal. S.P. Dom.* 1644–5, 46, 399; 1653–4, 195–6, 294.

18 W. Pope, *Life of Bishop Seth Ward*, 1697, 61–62; Hoare, *Mod. Wilts.* Salisbury, 459.

19 A. G. Matthews, *Walker Revised*, 14, 377, 380; *D.N.B.* s.v. Duppa.

20 Matthews, *Walker Revised*, 67, 133–4, 378; *Trans. Sar. Field Club*, i, 96–97, ii, 83; *D.N.B.* s.v. Henchman; Fletcher, 'Humphrey Henchman, Bp. of Salisbury', *W.A.M.* xlviii, 305–9.

21 A. G. Matthews, *Walker Revised*, 10, 112, 137, 372.

22 Ibid. 3–4, 47–48, 144, 341; *D.N.B.* s.v. Pearson; J. M. J. Fletcher, *Opuscula et Posthuma of John Gregory*; J. M. J. Fletcher, *The Boy Bishop at Salisbury and Elsewhere* (1921), 1–2.

vicars choral and lay vicars received payments from the Trustees for the Maintenance of Ministers in 1658 and 1659, though they had earlier taken part in the fighting against Parliament.[23]

THE RESTORATION

In 1660 the three surviving members of the residentiary chapter, Dean Bailey, Precentor Henchman, and Matthew Nicholas, now Dean of St. Paul's, set about restoring the broken institutions, worship, and discipline at the cathedral and of re-integrating their property. They held their first formal meeting with the larger chapter on 13 September, but were joined by only four prebendaries: John Earle the chancellor, John Ryves, Archdeacon of Berkshire, Alexander Hyde, and John Chappell.[24] The most immediate need was to fill the many vacancies. On the first day five new prebendaries were installed and by 22 September eighteen in all. Four new residentiaries were elected, including the chancellor, John Earle, Alexander Hyde, and two of the newly appointed prebendaries. A succentor was installed; vicars choral, lay vicars, and choristers were admitted.[25] Then, on 4 October, Henchman was elected and installed as bishop by royal nomination, following Bishop Duppa's translation to Winchester;[26] Thomas Hyde, Bishop Duppa's vicar-general and official, took Henchman's place in the residentiary chapter, and a third member of the Hyde family, Richard, became a prebendary and sub-dean.[27] Dean Bailey alone remained to preside over his reconstituted chapter until his death in 1667. In 1662 he wrote to the Earl of Clarendon that he had just returned from Salisbury to Oxford, having at Salisbury 'contracted the work of some weeks (in former times) into two days, owing to the sedulity of my brethren'.[28]

The restoration chapter seems to have been active and conscientious, working at first in harmony with both its bishops and deans. The first three bishops, Henchman, John Earle, and Alexander Hyde, who followed each other in quick succession, were all former members of the residentiary chapter and understood its problems; Henchman especially gave vigorous leadership. The fourth, Seth Ward, who was translated from Exeter in 1667, was one of the outstanding bishops of his time, a distinguished scientist and foundation member of the Royal Society. He took an active interest in the cathedral fabric and services, and contributed generously to paving the cloister and choir and to the new choir stalls. In 1668–9, when there was anxiety about the spire, he persuaded his friend, Sir Christopher Wren, to survey the cathedral and advise the chapter on how to strengthen it. He regularly attended the cathedral services twice daily with his household whenever he was in Salisbury; and so long as Ralph Brideoak, who had succeeded Richard Bailey as dean, remained there, his frequent presence and advice brought no conflict with the dean and chapter.[29] Episcopal visitations of the cathedral were made in 1661 by Bishop Henchman and in 1671 by Bishop Ward.[30] They suggest that the recovery, leasing, and repair of its property were among the main problems occupying the chapter's attention. Statutes published by Bishop Henchman after his visitation laid down that all leases of the prebends and other property must be approved by the bishop, dean, and chapter; that all chancels of churches and other buildings belonging to the chapter must be repaired within two years; that all houses in the close must be inspected annually and repaired within fifteen months; that a register of the customs, leases, and extents of all the prebends and common estates must be compiled and kept for reference in the cathedral muniment room.[31] By 1671 much progress had been made. Most of the property was apparently recovered fairly quickly. Pentecostal chapters had been reinstituted and were attended by large numbers of prebendaries who brought the leases and terriers of their prebends for registration.[32] In 1671 all the common property was in good repair, save the parsonage house at Bramshaw which had been burnt in the time of troubles.[33] All the fines from the fabric lands, amounting to £4,200, were spent on repairs of the cathedral fabric, to which the prebendaries also contributed £500 by a tax on their prebendal incomes. The repair and rebuilding of the houses in the close were vigorously undertaken. By 1670 £475 had been spent on the deanery and £775 on three other canonical houses.[34] Within 50 years or so the appearance of the close was largely transformed by the new style of domestic architecture. Much time and care was spent by the chancellor, Richard Drake, in arranging, cataloguing, indexing, and in many cases laboriously copying out the muniments.[35] This was partly to meet the need for complete titles of the recovered property; partly because of his genuine interest in the cathedral's

23 *W.A.M.* xlviii, 228–31; A. G. Matthews, *Walker Revised*, 15, 376, 379.

24 D. & C. Sar., Reg. Greenhill and Butler, f. 1.

25 D. & C. Sar., Reg. Butler, ff. 1–10; Robertson, *Sarum Close*, 199.

26 D. & C. Sar., Reg. Greenhill and Butler, ff. 5–8; *Cal. S.P. Dom.* 1660–1, 205, 305; 1661–2, 101; *Add.* 1660–85, 13.

27 D. & C. Sar., Reg. Greenhill and Butler, ff. 5, 8–9; *Cal. S.P. Dom.* 1660–1, 219; *Fasti Eccl. Sar.* ed. Jones, 428, 441.

28 Bodl., Tanner MS. 30, f. 108.

29 W. Pope, *Bp. Ward*, 62–63; *D.N.B.* s.v. Ward and Brideoak; J. M. J. Fletcher, 'Seth Ward, Bp. of Salisbury', *W.A.M.* xlix, 1–16.

30 D. & C. Sar., Reg. Greenhill and Butler, ff. 12–16; Sar. Dioc. Regy., Bp. Ward's Visitation Bk. 1671.

31 *Stat. Sar.* 418–38.

32 Ibid. 420–1; D. & C. Sar., Reg. Greenhill and Butler, ff. 35–38, 45–47, 51–54; *Cath. Com. 1st Rep.* [1822], pp. 418, 762–5, H.C. (1854), xxv; Bodl. Tanner MS. 143, ff. 259, 263.

33 Sar. Dioc. Regy., Bp. Ward's Visitation Bk. 1671, f. 9.

34 Bodl. Tanner MS. 143, ff. 259*a*, 263.

35 His Hist. Colls. and indexes are still in the Cath. muniment room.

Salisbury Cathedral, East Cloister, *c.* 1940

history and antiquities. The communar's accounts were kept with exemplary care in book form, with a single annual account in place of the four quarterly rolls. Drake prefaced his account of 1668–9 by Latin verses of his own composition, describing the traditional way in which the accounts were made up and the profits divided.[36] Much more attention was also paid to the library. A catalogue of the manuscripts was made soon after 1670, and since then there have been few losses.[37]

Worship and discipline at the cathedral seem to have been of a high standard compared with that of the 1630's. Drake, as the dean's *locum tenens*, insisted that vicars who wished to be absent from either of the two daily services must always ask leave and offer a reasonable excuse.[38] Sermons were frequent. A revised list of preaching turns was drawn up and enforced, and, at least while the court lived at Salisbury during the plague of 1665, two sermons a day were preached on Sundays, by the prebendaries in the presbytery in the morning, and by the residentiaries in the nave in the afternoon. In 1670 when Archbishop Sheldon sent his circular letter to cathedrals requiring the canons to celebrate communion on Sundays and holy days in person and not to leave it to their vicars, the dean and chapter replied that they had already begun to do so; the 52 Sundays of the year were divided up among the six residentiaries, the four dignitaries, the sub-dean, and the succentor, who were to officiate in turn.[39] Much money was spent on the organ, and a brilliant though temperamental organist, Michael Wise, succeeded Giles Tompkins in 1668.[40] The number of choristers was increased from six to seven. After a brief experiment of boarding them with Wise, the system of salaries was reinstituted, but on a higher scale than before the war.[41] In 1673 Edward Hardwick, a vicar choral, became head master of the grammar school in the close, and the great days of the school began.[42] Cope money was reinstituted and the proceeds ordered to be applied to the adornment of the church.[43] The chapter bought more plate for the altar, and gifts were received. The treasurer's inventory of 1684 shows a great improvement on that of 1671, when complaints were made that the church was but meanly provided with plate.[44] Walter Pope declared that in the early years of Seth Ward's episcopate the cathedral services were celebrated with 'exemplary piety, admirable decency, and celestial music', and that the church was kept so clean that it would be difficult to find sufficient dust to blot the superscription of a letter.[45]

After his visitation Bishop Ward attempted to deal with the anomaly by which all four dignitaries were bound by ancient statutes to 'continuous' residence, whilst they were not all admitted to the residentiary chapter. He declared that in future all four dignitaries must keep residence for three months a year, each being responsible for a quarter of the year, and, if absent, must pay a fine of £5 a month. As Dean Pierce soon pointed out, this brought down the dignitaries' residence to 'none at all' on payment of £15 a year.[46] It would, however, hardly have been possible to insist on the dignitaries keeping residence while at the same time refusing to grant them a canonical house or a share in the profits of residence; and there seems to have been no thought of increasing the number of residentiaries. In 1670 the chapter told Archbishop Sheldon that the average sum from the common fund (including fines) divided among the dean and six residentiaries was about £450 a year, which would give to each about £64.[47] The communar's accounts suggest, however, that this was an under-estimate. There was still much competition for the residentiary places, and the system of pre-election forbidden in 1635 was soon in force again, as were the royal letters of recommendation.[48] In fact, most residentiaries of the late 17th century seem to have been 'recommended' to the chapter in royal letters. When the bishop or others wished to obtain residentiary places for their kinsmen, friends, or chaplains they asked for royal letters to the chapter in their favour.[49] On one occasion, in 1674, the chapter held an election 'clandestinely' while Dean Brideoak was absent at Windsor with the king, but was speedily rebuked. The king directed that a regular election should be held in the dean's presence, in which he did not doubt that the chapter would comply with his recommendation; but he did not attempt to override the rule which required residentiaries to be chosen from the prebendaries.[50]

Bishop Ward kept the appointments to prebends as far as possible in his own hands, giving some to the poorly paid incumbents in market towns of the diocese where the influence of the dissenters was strongest,[51] a policy continued by Bishop Burnet. Otherwise Ward's appointments were most remarkable for the very large number given to his own relatives.[52] A cause of one of the bitterest, most dramatic, and most astonishing disputes in

36 Bodl. Rawlinson MS. B. 441, f. 1.

37 *W.A.M.* liii, 162–4.

38 D. & C. Sar., Reg. Greenhill and Butler, f. 70*b*.

39 *Stat. Sar.* 502–6, 510–14, 516–20.

40 *W.A.M.* xlviii, 224–5; Robertson, *Sarum Close*, 201–5.

41 Robertson, op. cit. 199–201; *W.A.M.* xlviii, 215.

42 Robertson, *Sarum Close*, 214–16.

43 *Stat. Sar.* 438–45.

44 Sar. Dioc. Regy., Bp. Ward's Visitation Bk. 1671, ff. 9, 13; *W.A.M.* xxxix, 43–46; Bodl. Tanner MS. 143, f. 225.

45 W. Pope, *Bp. Ward*, 62–63.

46 *Stat. Sar.* 444–9.

47 Bodl. Tanner MS. 143, f. 259.

48 D. & C. Sar., Reg. Greenhill and Butler, ff. 6, 28, 73–74; Reg. Frome and Prince, ff. 20–22, 33, 58–61, 66; *Cal. S.P. Dom.* 1671, 33; 1672, 322, 325; 1676–7, 163; 1677–8, 11–12; 1679–80, 507, 573, 581; 1680–1, 10.

49 Ibid. 1673–5, 483; 1676–7, 163; Hist. MSS. Com. *Var. Coll.* i, 373.

50 *Cal. S.P. Dom.* 1673–5, 276–8, 282.

51 See above, p. 45.

52 Cf. *W.A.M.* xlix, 10–11.

the cathedral's history was his grant of the rich prebend of Teignton Regis to his nephew, Thomas Ward. Thomas Pierce, who became dean in 1675, badly wanted it for his son, Robert, and maintained that the bishop had promised it to him.[53] Pierce was probably the most difficult dean with whom any bishop or chapter of Salisbury has been confronted. At first a Calvinist, he had turned Arminian during the Civil War, and proclaimed his views with a convert's zeal. As President of Magdalen College, Oxford, after the Restoration he gained a reputation for being 'high, proud, and mad'; he expelled a fellow, defied the Visitor, and was eventually forced to resign.[54] At Salisbury in the 1680's Archbishop Sancroft's view was that the dean's haughty and revengeful spirit was at the bottom of all the troubles which threw the cathedral life into confusion and undid much of the careful work of restoration of the previous 20 years.[55] Pierce wanted both arbitrary power over the cathedral and revenge against the bishop for the slight to his son. He therefore claimed that Salisbury was no ordinary cathedral but a royal free chapel directly subject to the king and exempt from the bishop's jurisdiction and visitation. This chapel had existed in the royal castle at Salisbury before the Norman Conquest. Since the dean had existed before the bishop and was immediately subject to the king, his jurisdiction over his chapter and its property was obviously greater than that of any bishop; it could best be described as a kind of archiepiscopal jurisdiction. The composition of 1392 which allowed episcopal visitation was void because it was popish.

The result of all this extraordinary historical research and invention was set out at first anonymously, then in formal petitions to the king protesting against the bishop's claim to collate to prebends, and asking the king to forbid the bishop's intended visitation of the cathedral in 1683 as an infringement of royal rights, and finally in a virulent printed pamphlet, *A Vindication of the King's Sovereign Right*.[56] The petitions were referred to Lord North, Keeper of the Great Seal, and Sir Robert Sawyer, the Attorney General, who pronounced strongly in the bishop's favour, and the king was advised to allow the bishop's visitation to proceed.[57] The visitation, however, served only to reveal the deep divisions, quarrels, and resentments in the cathedral body, so that Bishop Ward wrote in dismay to Archbishop Sancroft for advice and help. 'Matters are at such a crisis here (by the perversion of some persons) that it is very hard for the many wise and good men who are here to withstand the atheism, profaneness and debauchery visibly breaking out.'[58] The dean had won the allegiance of one residentiary canon, Francis Horton, and of two vicars choral, John Hopkins and William Powell, who seem to have been the most disreputable members of their body. In opposition were ranged all the other five residentiary canons, led by the precentor, Daniel Whitby, whom Dean Pierce described as 'our Protestant Embroiler, an eminent misleader of his brethren', and by Seth Ward, the bishop's nephew.[59] After his visitation the bishop became mentally ill with worry. The dean published further libellous pamphlets against him and stirred up the lay vicars to disregard his wishes.[60] The Bishop of Bristol, after visiting Salisbury, wrote to tell his archbishop that there was now a scandalous neglect of the services.[61] Relations between the dean and chapter also became steadily worse. In 1685 the five residentiaries petitioned the archbishop to prevent the dean from acting independently of his chapter, saying that their visitor, the bishop, was detained by sickness and could not protect them. All their complaints were confirmed by Geoffrey Frome, the chapter clerk, and defiantly admitted by the dean. He had kept the chapter seal for nine months while frequently absent from Salisbury, thus making it impossible for leases and other documents to be sealed. He had admitted a lay vicar and dismissed the vicar of the close (that is, the vicar choral with cure of souls in the close) on his own authority, and had ordered his acts as dean alone, without the chapter, to be registered in the chapter act book. He had refused to allow the customary annual election of a *custos munimentorum* and Masters of the Fabric from among the canons, but had kept both offices and all the fabric money in his own hands. He had presented no accounts of the fabric fund, and he had had a special key for the muniment chest made for himself.[62] Eventually the king and archbishop decided that the dean must be forced to submit and apologize to the bishop; that the chapter must have its privileges restored, and that a metropolitan visitation of the cathedral should be made by royal command to prevent further disorders.[63] These things were done, but a further proposal to issue a complete new set of statutes for the cathedral was abandoned. In July 1686 the dean asked the bishop for pardon and humbly begged restoration to his former favour and friendship. In the same month the archbishop's commissaries began their visitation. They made a solemn peace between bishop, dean, and canons, and the dean and chapter formally declared that their church was not a royal

53 Bodl. Tanner MS. 143, f. 46*b*.

54 *D.N.B.*

55 Bodl. Tanner MS. 143, f. 46*a*.

56 D. & C. Sar., Reg. Frome and Prince, ff. 75–76; Sar. Dioc. Regy., Fasti, ii, ff. 1, 10 sqq.; Bodl. Tanner MS. 143, ff. 51, 99, 103, 105, 149–56, 162, 170, 172, 192–9. *A Vindication of the King's Sovereign Right* was first printed in 1683, and reprinted in Rawlinson, *Hist. and Antiqs. of Salisbury Cath.* 1723.

57 D. & C. Sar., Reg. Frome and Prince, ff. 76–78; Bodl. Tanner MS. 89, ff. 157–8; 143, ff. 51, 147, 164.

58 Bodl. Tanner MS. 89, ff. 173, 234–5.

59 Ibid. ff. 87, 107, 211, 223, 232–5; for Whitby see *D.N.B.*

60 Bodl. Tanner MS. 143, ff. 185, 200, 230.

61 Ibid. 30, f. 51*a*.

62 Ibid. 143, ff. 87–98, 183, 202, 237, 241, 247, 250.

63 Ibid. f. 48.

chapel but a cathedral, and that the bishop had the right to visit every seven years according to the composition of 1392.[64]

The state of the cathedral as revealed in the archbishop's *detecta* of 1686 was, not unnaturally, less satisfactory than at Bishop Ward's first visitation of 1671, though efforts were being made to restore order. The rota of residence was apparently being observed for the most part, though there were some irregularities and two members of the chapter had dispensations from residence at their other benefices. The prebendaries complained that the residentiaries were not exercising their duties of hospitality to them. Prebendary Townson declared that, when he was present in the close eight times in the extreme heat of mid-June, Dr. Whitby and Dr. Lambert would not offer him a cup of small beer to refresh him. Communion was celebrated once a month instead of once a week as the canons of the Church of England directed. Canon Horton was said seldom to be present at the service, while two other canons had been absent last month, one (Seth Ward) because he had been officiating instead at the bishop's palace. The chapter did not often exact the duty of attending communion from the vicars choral, since nearly all served nearby cures, where they had to administer the sacrament and preach on Sundays. The choir seems on the whole to have been efficient. The six vicars choral and seven lay vicars provided five basses, four tenors, and four counter-tenors. No complaints were made of their skill in music, and they were all said normally to be present at each of the two daily services, though some sometimes came late or went early. Michael Wise received high praise for his skill as an organist, but was erratic in his attendances. The vicars did not all live in their proper houses in the close, but explained that some lay vicars were tradesmen in the city and lived at their shops.[65]

The settlement of the great dispute was followed in rapid succession by the Revolution (when James II stayed for a few nights at the bishop's palace, and three or four prebendaries were later deprived of their prebends as non-jurors),[66] and by the deaths of Bishop Ward in 1689 and of Dean Pierce in 1691. With the remarkable Gilbert Burnet, a Scot and latitudinarian, as its bishop, and Robert Woodward, a lawyer and good administrator, as its dean, the chapter entered on a new phase of its existence.

THE EIGHTEENTH CENTURY

Eighteenth-century English cathedral clergy have a bad name for torpor, slackness, resistance to change, worldliness, non-residence, and pluralism. At Salisbury such generalizations are not possible. The rules and customs of canonical residence were inherited from the past, and practically no change was made in them. Pluralism had been well established for centuries; most of the canons and prebendaries held at least one benefice with cure of souls outside the cathedral and an indefinite number of prebends at other cathedrals, but this was no more than their predecessors had done in the preceding 300 years. In some ways there was lively activity in the 18th-century close rather than torpor or quiet, and not all this activity was of a secular character.

The charge of torpor was probably most justified in constitutional matters, for there were few important developments and little legislation. The 18th-century bishops and chapter can hardly be blamed for failing to overhaul the mass of medieval statutes and customs. Worse was their failure to maintain the two useful institutions of episcopal visitation and Pentecostal chapters, by which supplementary statutes had been made and abuses corrected since the Reformation. No episcopal visitations were held at the cathedral between Bishop Burnet's visitation of 1697 and that of Bishop John Wordsworth in 1888, and no Pentecostal chapters have been traced between 1670 and 1813 save for an exceptional one in 1740. Nevertheless, some changes and corrections were still made by acts of the residentiary chapter, which met regularly to deal with the administrative business of the cathedral;[67] and for the more important matters the bishop was occasionally invited to attend either as a Visitor or prebendary. In the mid-18th century the chapter several times invited or appealed to Bishop Thomas Sherlock to determine its disputes, or to help in the interpretation and adaptation of ancient statutes.[68] Quarrelsomeness and divisions within the chapter had not died out with the 17th century, though there was apparently more readiness to ask for and accept the bishop's advice. In 1740 Joseph Sager, a residentiary canon, was judged before Bishop Sherlock as Visitor in a full Pentecostal chapter for misconduct and for dividing the revenues of the common fund unfairly.[69] Then, in the following year, the chapter asked the bishop's advice about their election of a new communar. Canon Wynn proposed a residentiary, Canon Whishaw, who was also a prebendary of Winchester cathedral, and the objection was raised that a statute of 1516 said that no canon of Salisbury who was also a residentiary at another cathedral could be communar, because the office required his continuous presence throughout the year. Bishop Sherlock declared that the office of communar no longer required continuous attendance, for its burdens were much lighter. The abolition of obits had removed one of his

64 Ibid. ff. 48*b*, 166*a*, 203, 207; D. & C. Sar., Reg. Frome and Prince, f. 90.

65 Bodl., Tanner MS. 143, ff. 178–81, 187, 189–90, 203–4, 208–9, 252, 295.

66 Hoare, *Mod. Wilts.* Salisbury, 490; W. H. Jones, *Salisbury* (Diocesan Hists. 1880), 252, 257–9, 259 n.; T. E. S. Clarke and H. C. Foxcroft, *Life of Burnet*, 301–4.

67 Some of these acts were printed in *Cath. Com. 1st Rep.* [1822], pp. 384–5, H.C. (1854), xxv.

68 Ibid. p. 418; below, nn. 69, 70, 74.

69 Sar. Reg. Sherlock, f. 19; D. & C. Sar., Reg. Frome, ff. 277–86.

responsibilities; he no longer had to supervise repairs on the common estates because repairs were now done by the tenants, and payment of commons was now made annually, not quarterly. If Canon Whishaw had to go to Winchester for part of the year, he could exercise his office by deputy during that time. But it was important that all six residentiaries should accept the office in turn.[70]

This decision is interesting in showing how the dean and chapter were now able to enjoy the fruits of their increasingly prosperous estates with much less effort than in previous centuries. Few attempts were made to raise the reserved rents, but increasingly large fines were received on the renewal of leases. These fines had now become much more valuable than the regular rents. This was recognized in 1813 when an isolated Pentecostal chapter declared that the 20 per cent. tax on the reserved rents of prebends and dignities for the fabric had become both burdensome and ineffectual, and imposed instead a 2½ per cent. tax on all fines for the renewal of leases, which was expected to bring in a considerably larger sum.[71]

A similar development was apparently taking place on the estates of the vicars choral, though the vicars were anxious to conceal it. Their attitude provides perhaps the most striking example of selfish opposition to change in the 18th-century cathedral. Leases granted by them after 1660 show that the reserved rents of all their estates had been raised in accordance with the award of 1624 to make up the annual stipends of the seven lay vicars to £20 each.[72] After this the rents were raised no farther, and the vicars choral, whose numbers were apparently reduced to five sometime after 1725,[73] shared the steadily rising fines. Throughout the 18th century they refused to consider increasing the lay vicars' stipends in any way, although pressed to do so by the chapter. Shortly before 1750 a dispute between the choral and lay vicars was brought before Bishop Sherlock, who decided that legally the lay vicars were only stipendiaries, and that the vicars choral could not be compelled to pay them more than was laid down in the agreement of 1624.[74] The chapter proposed that until the value of the estates should further increase the fifth choral vicar's place might be left vacant and his stipend used to pay an extra £5 a year to each of the lay vicars. The vicars choral readily agreed to the reduction of their numbers to four, but, on discovering that the reduction had not been registered as permanent in the chapter act book, refused to make the additional payments to the lay vicars and simply divided up the fifth stipend amongst themselves.[75] In 1793–4 the lay vicars made a last determined effort to assert their claims in formal petitions, first to the vicars choral and then to the dean and chapter.[76] They declared that they would be satisfied with the promised extra £5 a year and would cease to press for a share in the fines. In the meantime they employed the chapter clerk to search the muniments in support of their claims. The dean and chapter thought their request very reasonable, but the vicars choral unhesitatingly refused it.[77] The agreement of 1624 was finally produced, and convinced both chapter and vicars choral that legal right was on the side of the vicars choral to such an extent that the chapter even forbore to insist that the fifth choral vicar's place should be filled.[78] The attitude of the vicars to this long dispute is illustrated by two contemporary notebooks, one kept by Israel Vanderplank, for many years procurator of the vicars choral, the other by Robert Barret, a lay vicar, who called his account 'A Narrative of the Priest and Lay Vicars'.[79] Corporate feeling, now well developed among the lay vicars, is illustrated by the agreement of Highmore Skeats, a layman in the church for over 50 years, to join in their petition of 1793 in spite of his advanced age. He advised them about the past, telling them that 'the matter had often been on the carpet but always frustrated', and urged them not to have too high hopes.[80] Robert Barret wrote of 'the shameful Jesuiticall way of reasoning' of the vicars choral. He also attacked their competence, saying that they were no use in the choir, and totally incapable of singing the anthem or the service. 'Only one attends at a time unless profits are to be had.'[81] Allowance must be made for Robert Barret's prejudice, but it seems likely that the music and singing were coming to depend increasingly on the lay vicars and choristers. About 60 years later the dean and chapter stated that the four vicars choral then attended the church services a week each in turn, and appointed one of their number to be present on Sunday.[82]

The history of the choristers suggests quite a different picture of cathedral life. The choir was augmented, salaries were readily increased, new buildings were undertaken, new endowments acquired, and musical education and the grammar school flourished. The revenues began to improve about 1712, and in the following year the chapter decided to increase the number of boys to eight. The salaries of the two senior choristers were

70 D. & C. Sar., Act Bk. 1741–96, ff. 3–5.

71 *Stat. Sar.* 456–8.

72 Sar. Dioc. Regy., Vicars Choral Box, Acct. Bk. 1802, ff. 18–31.

73 They were still 6 in 1725: D. & C. Sar., Reg. Frome, ff. 163–4.

74 Sar. Dioc. Regy., Vicars Choral Box, Bk. of I. Vanderplank, f. 10.

75 Ibid. Bk. of R. Barret, f. 3.

76 Ibid. Bk. of I. Vanderplank, ff. 1–8.

77 Ibid. ff. 16, 22; Barret's Bk. f. 5; *Cath. Com. 1st Rep.* p. 386.

78 Sar. Dioc. Regy., Vicars Choral Box, I. Vanderplank's Bk. ff. 9–36; R. Barret's Bk. ff. 7–9.

79 Both books are in Sar. Dioc. Regy., Vicars Choral Box.

80 Sar. Dioc. Regy., Vicars Choral Box, R. Barret's Bk. at back, f. 2.

81 Ibid. at front, ff. 3–5, 7–11.

82 *Cath. Com. 1st Rep.* p. 387, cf. pp. 708–9.

raised to £12 a year each, the next two to £10, and the four juniors to £8 each.[83] The 18th-century choristers had good music teachers and instructors, drawn chiefly from the organists and lay vicars. They lived mostly at their own homes or in small boarding houses kept by widows in the city or close. On leaving the choir they were given an apprentice fee or money to help with their further education. Their endowment was increased in 1724 when an estate was bought at Tilshead for £900; five-sixths of the revenues from it went to the choristers, and one-sixth to the cathedral library.[84]

The 18th-century deans and canons included a remarkable variety of men. Among the deans were John Clarke (1728–57), a distinguished mathematician and younger brother of Samuel Clarke, the metaphysician; Thomas Greene (1757–80), son of the Bishop of Norwich, who was said to be artistic and finical, but who was also apparently efficient; and Rowney Nowel (1780–6), uncle of Lord Wentworth, whose appointment seems to have been mainly due to family and political reasons.[85] They seem on the whole, however, to have been less distinguished than their predecessors. From 1675 until 1954 no Dean of Salisbury has been promoted to a bishopric, whereas in earlier centuries this was very usual. The canons and prebendaries included many bishops' kinsmen, and others of aristocratic birth, such as Robert Sherard, a residentiary from 1758, who in 1770 succeeded to the Earldom of Harborough.[86] Much pressure was put on the bishops by the political parties to give prebends to their nominees. Burnet, however, made his own decisions. Among his most interesting appointments were those of Peter Allix, a learned French protestant, to the treasurership, and of several mathematicians and theologians to prebends, including John Craig, author of *Theologiae Christianae Principia Mathematica*, a leading exponent of the new attempts to apply the rules of science and reason to theology.[87] Other canons and prebendaries took part in the theological controversies of the time. Joseph Butler, author of the *Analogy of Religion, Natural and Revealed, to the Constitution and Course of Nature*, one of the most influential books of the century, was prebendary of Yetminster Prima from 1721 to 1738, and John Bampton, founder of the Bampton lectures at Oxford, was a residentiary. Towards the end of the century Charles Daubeny, Archdeacon of Salisbury, defended High Church principles against both protestant dissent and Roman Catholicism in his *Guide to the Church*.[88] Particularly in the early 18th century the chapter made efforts to improve the cathedral library.[89] The catalogue of manuscripts was revised, and Canon Isaac Walton, son of the *piscator*, and Canon Wyatt between them gave £150 to appoint a librarian. Their gift formed part of the purchase money of the Tilshead estate in 1724, from which a salary of about £7 or £8 a year was henceforth paid to a librarian.[90] Shortly before this the chapter had tried unsuccessfully to recover some of the cathedral manuscripts which had found their way to the Bodleian Library.[91] Canons and prebendaries continued to take a lively interest in the cathedral's history and muniments. Several more historical collections, including those of Canon Isaac Walton, were compiled from the muniments and handed down with Drake's collections. The antiquaries, Thomas Tanner and Richard Rawlinson, had permission to work in the muniment room, with the result that many copies of Salisbury documents are now available in their manuscript collections at the Bodleian.[92] Rawlinson published his *History and Antiquities of the Church of Salisbury* in 1723, Francis Price, a clerk of the works, his architectural *Descriptions of the Cathedral* in 1753 and 1774, and William Dodsworth, the cathedral verger, his *Guide to Salisbury Cathedral* in 1792 and his *Historical Account of the Episcopal See and Cathedral Church* in 1814.[93]

Other interests of the cathedral clergy were music and hospitality. Salisbury in the 18th century was at the height of its fame as a centre of music and fashion, and the cathedral clergy and choir played a leading part in the many musical activities. Interest in the cathedral music was shown by the installation of a magnificent new organ in 1710 over the entrance to the choir.[94] In addition music meetings were held at the canons' houses in the close; concerts were organized in the city by the lay vicars and cathedral organists, and music festivals were held annually in the cathedral from about 1744 until 1787.[95] All these activities were supported by the gay, intelligent, and fashionable society which had its

[83] D. & C. Sar., Reg. Frome, f. 90; Robertson, *Sarum Close*, 228–9.

[84] Robertson, op. cit. 230–2, 246–7; *Endowed Char. Wilts.* 'The Choristers' School, Salisbury', H.C. 255–1, p. 3 (1907), lxi (1); D. & C. Sar., Reg. Frome, ff. 157–8; *W.A.M.* xlviii, 210.

[85] *D.N.B.* s.v. Clarke, John, and Greene, Thomas; *Correspondence of Geo. III*, ed. Fortescue, v, no. 2984.

[86] D. & C. Sar., Act Bk. 1741–96, ff. 99–100, 215–17. He resigned his residentiary place in 1773.

[87] *Fasti Eccl. Sar.* ed. Jones, 349, 379; T. E. S. Clarke and H. C. Foxcroft, *Life of Burnet*, 293–4.

[88] *Fasti Eccl. Sar.* ed. Jones, 166, 403, 435; *D.N.B.*

[89] It had recently received an important legacy of books from Bp. Seth Ward: *W.A.M.* xlix, 12.

[90] *W.A.M.* liii, 163; D. & C. Sar., Reg. Frome, ff. 157–8; *Endowed Char. Wilts.* H.C. 255–1, p. 3 (1907), lxi.

[91] *W.A.M.* liii, 160–2; Hist. MSS. Com. *Var. Coll.* i, 384; copy of lost letter of Thomas Hyde, Bodley's librarian, to Dean of Salisbury, 1689, kept at p. 155 of annotated copy of Macray's *Annals of Bodleian* (1890) at Bodl. Libr.

[92] e.g. Bodl. Tanner MSS. 30, 89, 143, 268, 327; Rawlinson MS. C. 421.

[93] He was helped by Hen. Hatcher, then collecting material, which was later used in the Salisbury vol. of Hoare, *Mod. Wilts.*: W. Dodsworth, *Hist. Acct.* (1814), p. viii.

[94] C. Wordsworth and D. H. Robertson, 'Hist. of the Organ', *W.A.M.* xlviii, 226.

[95] Hoare, *Mod. Wilts.* Salisbury, 585–6; Robertson, *Sarum Close*, 237, 245–7.

centre in the cathedral close and which took much interest in the cathedral sermons and services. Large congregations attended on Sundays, on festivals, and in Lent.[96]

The drastic dealings of the 18th-century bishops and chapter with their cathedral fabric also help to contradict the idea of the period as being one of slackness and torpor. A description of the church frequently attributed to Daniel Defoe in his *Tour of the Whole Island of Britain* in the early mid-18th century says that 'the choir had been made to resemble a theatre painted white with golden panels and groups and garlands of roses and other flowers intertwined round the top of the stalls' and that the episcopal throne 'would make a fine theatrical decoration'.[97] In fact Defoe's opinion was very different. In 1724 he wrote that 'the Painting in the Choir is mean and more like the ordinary Method of common Drawing Room or Tavern painting than that of a Church'; the third edition of his book in 1742 agreed that the church 'now makes a better appearance than it has done'; but in 1748 in the fourth edition he said that it was 'hurt by the paltry old Painting in and over the Choir, and the White washing lately done, wherein they, very stupidly, have everywhere drawn black lines, to imitate Joints of Stone'.[98] Next, in 1758, the chapter decided to take down the spire and tower of the belfry, and the southern part of the library, on the ground that the whole library was too heavy to be properly supported by the cloisters; in 1762 six bells from the belfry were ordered to be sold, only two being reserved for the church's use.[99] In 1778 and 1779 the cathedral was closed for nearly two years while the choir was lengthened, the seats in the nave taken away, and pews or closets with galleries over them made on each side of the choir behind the stalls. The object was to make it possible to deliver sermons as well as to hold morning and evening prayers in the choir. Previously the whole congregation had moved from the choir to the nave for the Sunday sermon. The Earl of Radnor now had the inside Hungerford Chapel moved into the choir to serve as his family pew.[1] Finally, between 1789 and 1792 the most drastic changes were made, on the initiative of Bishop Shute Barrington, by the fashionable architect, James Wyatt, whose aim was to achieve vistas and light. The 13th-century choir screen was removed; most of the remaining medieval stained glass was broken up and the lead sold; clear glass was put in its place; the Lady Chapel was thrown open to the church and the monuments were moved about. Outside, the Beauchamp and Hungerford chapels and the 13th-century belfry were pulled down. The belfry was now regarded as a useless structure which blocked the view of the cathedral from the High Street gate and gave opportunities for carousal in its ale house. The ground of the churchyard was drained and levelled, the gravestones buried, and for the future the cloister garth was to be the cathedral cemetery. In 1792 George III, his queen, and six princesses attended the reopening of the cathedral and admired the 'improvements'.[2]

THE NINETEENTH CENTURY

In the early 19th century, particularly from about 1815 until 1840, the chapter passed through one of the most dangerous periods of its history, comparable in threats to its existence with those of the Reformation and Commonwealth. The chief cause was the failure of the Established Church to provide for the spiritual needs of the growing industrial towns. Criticism concentrated on the immense and supposedly increasing wealth of the higher clergy, some of it drawn from valuable industrial property, and on the lives of leisure lived by many canons and prebendaries.[3] Such criticism may have carried less weight against a chapter such as Salisbury, which drew its revenues mainly from agricultural land and tithes in counties little affected by the Industrial Revolution. Nevertheless, feeling rose high against all chapters, and the result was intervention by Parliament in the affairs of the Church. The biggest changes in revenues and organization ever made in the long history of Salisbury chapter were imposed by the Cathedrals Act of 1840. In comparison the Reformation changes appear conservative in the extreme. Yet continuity in cathedral life was maintained. Moreover, the survival of the cathedrals was due not solely to the effectiveness of parliamentary intervention, but largely to reforms and new ideas of the purpose of a cathedral expressed from within. Administrative reforms had already begun in the late Georgian Church, and the influence of the Oxford movement became powerful at the cathedral in the late 1830's.

The first two of the four royal commissions which investigated conditions at the cathedrals in the 19th century were concerned almost solely to discover how large a part of their revenues could reasonably be taken from them to establish new parishes in the industrial towns and to supplement the stipends of the poorer parish clergy. The first commission, inquiring into Ecclesiastical Revenues and Patronage, concluded that the net income of the whole church was under £3,500,000 a year, of which the bishoprics had about £157,000,

[96] Hoare, *Mod. Wilts.* Salisbury, 580–4.

[97] W. H. Jones, *Salisbury* (Diocesan Hists. S.P.C.K. 1880), 269; Robertson, *Sarum Close*, 224–5; J. Truby, *Glories of Salisbury Cath.* 20; J. R. H. Moorman, *Hist. of Engl. Church*, p. 288. The source of this quotation has not been traced.

[98] *Tour of the Whole Island of Britain*, 1st edn. 1724, i, 30; 3rd edn. 1742, i, 276; 4th edn. 1748, i, 326–8.

[99] D. & C. Sar., Act Bk. 1741–96, ff. 131–2, 164.

[1] Ibid. ff. 242, 250–2, 276; Hoare, *Mod. Wilts.* Salisbury, 531; *W.A.M.* xxxix, 51–52; *Cath. Com. 1st Rep.* p. 398.

[2] D. & C. Sar., Act Bk. 1741–96, ff. 319, 337–9, 346, 348, 357–9, 362–3; Hoare, *Mod. Wilts.* Salisbury, 540–7; W. Dodsworth, *Guide to Sar. Cath.* 31–43; J. M. J. Fletcher, 'The Old Belfry', *W.A.M.* xlvii, 612, 614–16.

[3] W. L. Mathieson, *Engl. Church Reform, 1815–40.*

and the cathedral and collegiate churches about £284,000; the second, investigating Ecclesiastical Duties and Revenues, decided that the most drastic transfers of cathedral property to a central Ecclesiastical Commission could produce only about £134,000 a year for use in the parishes.[4] Salisbury was among the chapters whose revenues were tending to decrease, because of the agricultural depression.[5] From being one of the richest English chapters in the Middle Ages it had by 1835 become one of the poorest, at least in the yield of its common fund. On a three-years' average the annual income from Salisbury's common fund was said to be about £3,176 gross or £2,800 net, about £2,000 of the gross income coming from fines, about £800 from reserved rents, about £150 from interest on investments, and the remainder from other small sources.[6] On a seven-years' average it was rather higher and allowed an annual income of about £556 to the dean and about £500 to each of the six residentiary canons.[7] Among cathedrals of the Old Foundation, only the common funds of Lichfield and York were smaller than this.[8] The revenues from the separate estates of dignities and prebends were even more variable and uncertain because leases were fewer and fines paid less often. During the three years ending in 1831 the prebendary of Hurstbourne and Burbage received only £50 a year in rents with a £15 fine, averaging an additional £5 a year; and the prebendary of the 'golden' prebend of Teignton Regis had only his regular income of £248 a year net in rents, tithes, woods, and dividends with fines of £330 spread over the three years. Yet in the same period the dean had an average annual income of about £2,679.[9] Among deans of the Old Foundation only those of St. Paul's and of Lincoln had higher incomes, while at Salisbury he was by far the richest member of the chapter. The treasurer, who was also a residentiary, came next with an average of about £1,500 a year; the chancellor and precentor, who were non-resident, had about £1,000 and £750 a year respectively, but this was drawn almost entirely from a few large fines, which would not recur for some time; their regular annual income from reserved rents still amounted for the chancellor to only £27 net, and for the precentor to £62 net.[10] The same difficulties apply to any attempt to draw conclusions about the revenues of the vicars choral. For the three years their fines averaged £37, and their annual revenues were given as about £437 gross or £243 net, allowing about £60 a year to each of the four vicars in addition to their commons money from the dean and chapter.[11] In other years, however, the state of the vicars' revenues was doubtless quite different.

The vicars choral were the only class for whom the Commissioners recommended increased stipends, so that they need no longer hold other benefices at a distance from the cathedral. The Commissioners thought, however, that the vicars' corporations should be dissolved and their property surrendered.[12] These last proposals met with so much opposition that they were eventually dropped from the Cathedrals Act, which declared only that 'minor canons' (a name then considered to be more suitable than 'vicars choral') should receive not less than £150 a year and hold no benefices more than 6 miles from the cathedral. For the chapters, drastic confiscations of revenues were ordered. All the separate estates of Salisbury's dignities and prebends were to be transferred to the Ecclesiastical Commission and their patronage to the bishop, subject only to the safeguarding of existing interests. Two of the six residentiary canonries were to be dissolved when their holders died, and their shares in the common fund paid to the Ecclesiastical Commission. The remaining common property was expected to provide annual incomes of about £1,000 for the dean, who was to reside for at least eight months a year, and about £500 for each of the four residentiary canons residing for at least three months a year. The churches belonging to the common fund might still be given by the chapter to its own members, to non-residentiary canons, to minor canons, or to others with at least five years' service in the diocese. The close chapter was to lose its right of electing residentiaries, who were to be nominated by the bishop, while the Crown kept the right of appointing the dean by letters patent. As a concession to those who opposed the abolition of all non-resident canons or prebendaries the bishop was allowed to appoint honorary non-resident canons and dignitaries so long as none of them received any emolument from his office. Lastly, the chapter was required to propose to their visitor for his approval alterations in its statutes to make them consistent with its changed constitution. The altered statutes were then to be submitted to the Ecclesiastical Commission and, if approved, laid before the queen in council.[13]

The chapter was thus far more firmly subjected to external control by Parliament, Ecclesiastical Commission, and bishop than it had ever been before. Its constitution had been altered and a

[4] Ibid. 112; *Eccl. Duties and Revenues Com. 2nd Rep.* H.C. 86, p. x, App. xi, p. 32 (1836), xxxvi.

[5] *Eccl. Revenues and Patronage Com. Rep.* H.C. 54, p. vii, Table ii, p. 23 (1835), xxxii.

[6] Ibid. Table ii, p. 22.

[7] *Eccl. Duties and Revenues Com. 2nd Rep.* App. iv, pp. 25–26.

[8] Ibid. *Eccl. Revenues and Patronage Com. Rep.* Table ii, pp. 10–26.

[9] Ibid. Table iii, pp. 64–69; *Eccl. Duties and Revenues Com. 2nd Rep.* App. viii, p. 27.

[10] *Eccl. Revenues and Patronage Com. Rep.* Table iii, pp. 64–65.

[11] Ibid. Table ii, pp. 24–25.

[12] *Eccl. Duties and Revenues Com. 2nd Rep.* p. 10; *4th Rep.* H.C. 387, p. 15 (1836), xxxvi; *5th Rep.* H.C. 66, pp. 5, 10–11 (1837–8), xxviii.

[13] Cathedrals Act, 3 & 4 Vic. c. 113.

large part of its revenues confiscated on the recommendation of men with very little knowledge of its history, purpose, or responsibilities. The slackness and conservatism of the early 19th-century chapter, like those of the 18th-century chapter, seem to have been exaggerated by its critics. Throughout the period there were some canons at Salisbury alive to their responsibilities and interested in the needs of the Church, though they did not make any big changes until after the visits of the royal commissioners. The commissioners remarked that the cathedral fabric had been kept in sound repair by the chapter's efforts and contributions, although the fabric revenues had become quite inadequate.[14] The grammar school had declined after the retirement of Dr. Skinner in 1801, partly owing to an alarming fall in the choristers' revenues, which meant that there was little competition for the post of head master. Throughout the inquiries of the royal commissioners the dean was Hugh Nicholas Pearson, whose special interests were in the spread of Christianity overseas, particularly in India. In 1836 Thomas Burgess was succeeded as bishop by Edward Denison, one of the youngest bishops Salisbury has ever had, a Fellow of Merton, who was strongly influenced by the Oxford Movement. He persuaded Walter Kerr Hamilton, another Fellow of Merton and his curate at St. Peter's-in-the-East, Oxford, to come to Salisbury, where he made him successively a residentiary canon and treasurer in 1841 and precentor in 1843.[15] Hamilton had been brought up as an evangelical but had gradually come under tractarian influence at Oxford. He had energy, vision, and deep religious conviction. In 1855 he succeeded Denison as bishop. Together they were the outstanding figures in the movement for cathedral reform at Salisbury in the mid-19th century.

Hamilton's appointment as precentor gave him authority to suggest reforms in the cathedral services and choir. He found that Holy Communion was celebrated only on the first Sunday in the month, on great festivals, and on Assize Sundays after the morning service at 10.30. He introduced an additional celebration on Sundays at 8 a.m. which he nearly always took himself. He revived the daily early morning service; persuaded the dean to arrange for a Sunday afternoon sermon in the choir in the summer months, himself took over from a vicar choral the preaching on festivals,[16] and ordered that the cathedral music should always be arranged beforehand by the canon in residence and the organist.[17] About 1851, new and more stringent rules of attendance were drawn up for the lay vicars, and fines were imposed for absence. In order to augment the choir three supernumerary laymen were appointed and paid by the chapter. Altogether, by 1854 the dean and chapter were spending £281 a year from their common fund on the supernumeraries and on increasing the seven lay vicars' stipends to £50 or £60 a year each.[18] The vicars choral had triumphantly maintained their claim to pay the laymen only £20 a year each, and since the investigation of their revenues in 1835 the chapter had ceased to expect them to contribute more. It apparently also forbore to insist on their regular attendance at the choral services, though Canon Hamilton urged that at least two of the four should be required to take a full part in each service.[19] He was particularly interested in the choristers, and played an important part in the struggle to reform their school in the close.[20] The choristers' property had now greatly improved in value. It was already bringing in about £530 a year, and the chapter expected it would soon yield about £800 a year. As the revenues rose they proposed gradually to increase the number of choristers to sixteen.[21]

Both Denison and Hamilton did much to make the cathedral a centre of education for the diocese,[22] and to restore the fabric. The restoration of the cloisters was begun in Bishop Denison's time; and Bishop Hamilton initiated the restoration of the chapter house in his predecessor's memory.[23] In 1849 the nave was first opened to the public free of charge between 10.15 a.m. and 4 p.m., and from 1865 visitors were also allowed to see the choir, chapter house, and cloisters for a charge of 6*d.* payable to the fabric fund.[24] Since then the throng of visitors to the cathedral has steadily increased.

The progress of the revival at Salisbury is well illustrated in the reports of the royal commission appointed in 1852 to inquire into the state of cathedral and collegiate churches. The dean and chapter's replies about the work then being done were satisfactory, their returns on the historical development of their constitution were the most careful and detailed of any,[25] and their suggestions for further developments at the cathedral among the most interesting. The returns, compiled by Canon Hamilton with the approval of Henry Parr Hamilton, who had succeeded to the deanery in 1850, entailed much research and helped to reveal how ruthlessly the framers of the 1840 Act had changed the constitution of the cathedral without adequate historical knowledge. The attitude of

[14] *Eccl. Revenues and Patronage Com. Rep.* Table ii, p. 23; cf. *Cath. Com. 1st Rep.* p. 396.

[15] *D.N.B.*; H. P. Liddon, *Walter Kerr Hamilton* (1869).

[16] Liddon, op. cit. p. 24; Sar. Dioc. Regy., Chapter Min. Bk. 1834–51, f. 229; *Sar. Dioc. Gaz.* xxiii, 121, 141.

[17] Robertson, *Sarum Close*, 279–80.

[18] *Cath. Com. 1st Rep.* pp. 376–7, 387, 392–3, 420–2, 727.

[19] Ibid. pp. 708–9.

[20] See *V.C.H. Wilts.* v.

[21] Robertson, *Sarum Close*, 284–5, 288–9; *Cath. Comm. 1st Rep.* pp. xxxiv, 388–92, 611.

[22] See above, p. 66, and chapter on Education in *V.C.H. Wilts.* v.

[23] *Cath. Com. 1st Rep.* p. 396; *Salisbury Cath. Com. Rep.* [C 4237], App. p. 4, H.C. (1884–5), xxi; Robertson, *Sarum Close*, 287.

[24] Robertson, op. cit. 293, 302; Sar. Dioc. Regy., Chapter Min. Bk. 1834–51, f. 229; *Cath. Com. 1st Rep.* pp. xlvi, 394.

[25] *Cath. Com. 1st Rep.* pp. 363–424.

the Cathedral Commissioners of the 1850's was very different. Their object was to increase the usefulness of the cathedrals, and promote the 'high and holy purposes' for which they had been founded.[26] Many of the proposals, however, including some by Canon Hamilton in his famous *Letter on Cathedral Reform*[27] and in his replies to the Commissioners, had their origin more in ideas of what was thought to be the purpose and work of a cathedral in the early centuries of the Church rather than in the Middle Ages, when it had existed chiefly to provide the constant round of services within its walls. A new idea of the purpose of a cathedral was developed. The object now was to make it the diocesan centre of religious life, education, and music, with the chapter acting as the bishop's council in diocesan work and administration, and the cathedral clergy taking a leading part in ecclesiastical work in the city, directing educational, musical, pastoral, and charitable activities and attending the meetings of the increasing number of church societies. For this Canon Hamilton declared that it would be necessary to enforce constant residence of at least nine months a year on the residentiary canons as well as on the dean and vicars choral, and to forbid them to hold other benefices with their canonries.[28] It was thought that the biggest breach made in the medieval constitution by the disendowment of the non-resident canons might be partly repaired by bringing them into closer connexion with the cathedral through more frequent meetings of the greater chapter, the revival of the annual Pentecostal chapter, and their regular performance of their annual preaching turns at the cathedral. It was claimed that an active and scholarly body of non-residents could still do valuable work as advisers of the close chapter, while away from the cathedral they would widen its basis and strengthen its links with the diocese.[29] Most of the non-resident canons were now beneficed clergy of the diocese. Bishop Denison had made a practice of appointing rural deans of the diocese and scholar clergy interested in local ecclesiastical history; among his nominations were William Dansey, author of *Horae Decanicae Rurales*, and William Palmer, author of *Origines Liturgicae*, a book which was influential in reviving interest in the history of the liturgy and prayer book.[30] Other constitutional changes proposed to the Commissioners seemed to favour a greater approximation to the simpler centralized constitutions of cathedrals of the New Foundation. It was urged that the dean should be given greater power over the chapter, that the bishop should have more power and rights at the cathedral, that the minor corporation of vicars choral should be dissolved and its members brought under closer control by the dean and chapter, and that the number of lay vicars should be doubled.[31]

Obviously all these proposals required more money than had been left to the cathedral by the Act of 1840, and the Commissioners and chapter hoped to obtain more profits from the remaining estates by discontinuing the old system of granting beneficial leases, and by more modern methods of estate management.[32] A statute of 1851 had given facilities for the voluntary enfranchisement of leasehold estates and the purchase of leasehold rights by the chapters,[33] but opinion at Salisbury was in favour of vesting all the property for a time in the hands of a central commission, for more profitable management, on condition that the resulting increased revenues should be used for the chapter's purposes and not paid to the Ecclesiastical Commission as was ordered in 1851.[34] In particular it was thought desirable that the residentiaries should have larger and regular incomes, and the Cathedral Commissioners agreed that if canons were to be expected to reside for nine months a year and to give up their other benefices their income should be raised to £750 and that of the dean to £1,500.[35]

No legislation resulted from the Commissioners' reports, but they drew attention to the chapter's work and problems. In 1855 a further Order in Council arranged that the annual incomes of the residentiaries should be maintained at £500 by the Ecclesiastical Commission.[36] Then in 1861 the dean and chapter surrendered the property of the common and fabric funds (apart from their houses in the close) to the Ecclesiastical Commission in return for an annual payment of £4,200, until they should be re-endowed with estates yielding an equivalent regular income, and a lump sum of £10,000 to restore the cathedral fabric.[37] Shortly afterwards, in 1868, the corporation of vicars choral also surrendered their property to the Commission in return for an annual payment of £960 and a lump sum of £1,200; but it was unable to obtain any promise of future re-endowment with landed property.[38] In 1875 the dean and chapter were re-endowed with property in Stratford-sub-Castle, Bemerton, Milford, Winterbourne

26 Ibid. p. 1.

27 First pub. 1853, reprinted by him as bp. with a pastoral letter, 1855.

28 W. K. Hamilton, *Letter on Cathedral Reform* (1853), 14, 26–28; *Cath. Com. 1st Rep.* pp. 610–11; Liddon, *W. K. Hamilton*, 30–32.

29 *Cath. Com. 1st Rep.* pp. xxxi–xxxii, 611–12; *3rd Rep.* [1936], pp. vii, viii, xvii, xxiv, 18 H.C. (1854–5), xv; Hamilton, *Letter on Cath. Reform* (1853), 24, 31.

30 *Fasti Eccl. Sar.* ed. Jones, 363, 393; *D.N.B.*; *Cath. Com. 1st Rep.* p. xxxii.

31 *Cath. Com. 1st Rep.* pp. 610–11, 709–10; *3rd Rep.* pp. viii, xii, xiii, xx; Hamilton, *Letter on Cath. Reform*, 13, 24, 26.

32 *Cath. Com. 1st Rep.* pp. l–li; *3rd Rep.* pp. xxi–xxiv.

33 Episcopal and Capitular Estates Act, 14 & 15 Vic. c. 104.

34 *Cath. Com. 1st Rep.* pp. 610–12, 621–2, 642–4; Hamilton, *Letter on Cath. Reform*, 8–12, 16–17, 32, 35.

35 *Cath. Com. 3rd Rep.* p. xxii.

36 *Lond. Gaz.* p. 541, Order in Council, 8 Feb. 1855.

37 Ibid. p. 4075, 11 Oct. 1861.

38 Ibid. p. 2791, 14 May 1868; Sar. Dioc. Regy., Vicar Choral Box, Min. Bk. s.a. 1864–8.

Gunner, Figheldean, Laverstock, Clarendon, and the parish of St. Thomas, Salisbury, which was expected to provide them with a regular income of about £4,700 a year. Of this £3,000 was to be set aside for the stipends of the dean and canons, and the remaining £1,700 with the income from their property in the close, used for the cathedral services and fabric and for other liabilities. Any surplus was to be accumulated for making good deficiencies in subsequent years.[39]

From 1863 to 1876 the restoration of the cathedral had been proceeding under the direction of Sir Gilbert Scott. The grant of £10,000 from the Ecclesiastical Commission proved completely inadequate. In 20 years over £82,000 was spent on the west front, the Lady Chapel, transepts and choir, and on the installation of heating. Much of the money was raised by subscription and gifts, including a new organ from Miss Chafyn-Grove.[40]

By the 1880's the big changes and experiments were over and the following period was one of consolidation and of adaptation to changed conditions. Under its scholarly and devout bishops, George Moberly and John Wordsworth, and with learned, able, and vigorous residentiaries such as Dean Boyle, Archdeacon Lear, and Chancellor Swayne,[41] the chapter reached a new peak of spiritual prestige. In addition to their cathedral duties, the clergy were taking a leading part in every kind of ecclesiastical activity of the city and diocese. Among the residentiaries in 1884 were two archdeacons of the diocese, the chancellor, who was secretary of the Diocesan Board of Education, and the treasurer, who was secretary of the Board of Foreign Missions. The precentorship was held by the dean, an arrangement favoured by Bishop Moberly, but not by Bishop Wordsworth.[42] Of the vicars choral, one was vice-principal of the Theological College; another religious instructor of the choristers; the third, cathedral librarian and parish priest of the close, and the fourth curate of Stratford-sub-Castle.[43] The expansion of the choir and of other cathedral activities continued. By 1885 there were 18 choristers and 4 supernumerary laymen in addition to the 7 lay vicars. The stipends of the lay vicars had been raised from chapter funds to about £93 and that of the organist to £150 a year.[44] The chancellor's divinity lectures were revived in 1894.[45] Careful catalogues were made of the printed books in the cathedral library by S. M. Lakin, the librarian and vicar choral, and of the manuscripts by E. Maunde Thompson of the British Museum;[46] catalogues of the muniments were soon to be made by the bishop's brother, Canon Christopher Wordsworth. Non-resident canons led the way in the study of local history and liturgy. Canon William Henry Rich Jones published his important *Fasti Ecclesiae Sarisberiensis* between 1879 and 1883, and his edition of the cathedral statutes in collaboration with Canon Dayman in 1883. Rather later Canon Christopher Wordsworth's immense output of historical and liturgical work encouraged the growing interest in the cathedral's history and in the medieval Use of Salisbury which has continued into the 20th century. In 1888 Bishop Wordsworth held the first visitation of the cathedral since 1697. No corrections were found necessary, though changes were suggested and earnestly discussed. At the end the bishop paid tribute to the whole cathedral body.[47] A few years earlier the royal commission, appointed in 1879, had commented in similar terms in its final report on the immense change which had taken place generally in the cathedrals since the 1830's and in the feeling with which they were regarded by lay people. Services had been improved and multiplied and attracted public interest in a way which 50 years earlier could scarcely have been anticipated as possible; the origin and idea of cathedrals had been more studied and understood; the capitular body was interested in the whole diocese, and the diocese had claims on the chapter.[48]

Nevertheless, there were still, as at all periods in the cathedral's history, frictions and jealousies within the cathedral body, and constitutional problems to be solved. The vicars choral were restive and jealous under the chapter's control and resented their description as 'inferior clergy'. The dean and chapter proposed the dissolution of the minor corporation as the only means of giving them proper control over the vicars.[49] At the same time the non-resident canons felt that the dean was denying them their just privileges as members of the greater chapter. In 1879 29 non-residents signed a petition to Dean Hamilton for the revival of the annual Pentecostal chapter, according to the recommendations of both dean and chapter and Cathedral Commission in 1854, but the dean refused to consider it. In 1880 a long statement laid before the Cathedral Commission the various ways in which the non-residents thought they should be allowed to take part in the cathedral's work. Their claims received some support within the close chapter from Chancellor

39 *Lond. Gaz.* p. 2582, Order in Council, 13 May 1875.

40 *Cath. Com. Final Rep.* [C 4371], pp. 41–43, H.C. (1884–5), xxi; Robertson, *Sarum Close*, 287, 303; *W.A.M.* xlviii, 226.

41 *D.N.B.* s.v. Moberly, Wordsworth, Boyle; C. A. E. Moberly, *Dulce Domum*; E. W. Watson, *Life of Bp. John Wordsworth*; G. D. Boyle, *Recollections of Dean of Salisbury*; F. Lear, 'Reminiscences', *Sar. Dioc. Gaz.* xxiii; *Salisbury Cath. Com. Rep.* (1884–5), pp. 20–22.

42 *Salisbury Cath. Com. Rep.* (1884–5), p. 3; *Stat. Sar.* 480.

43 *Salisbury Cath. Com. Rep.* (1884–5), p. 3.

44 Robertson, *Sarum Close*, 309; *Endowed Char. Wilts.* (1907), p. 4; *Salisbury Cath. Com. Rep.* (1884–5), p. 4; *Cath. and Coll. Churches (Lay Vicars and Clerks)*, H.C. 428, p. 539 (1876), lviii.

45 *Stat. Sar.* 508.

46 E. M. Thompson and S. M. Lakin, *Cat. of Salisbury Cath. Libr.*

47 *Stat. Sar.* 489.

48 *Cath. Com. Final Rep.* p. 16.

49 Cf. ibid. p. 4; *Salisbury Cath. Com. Rep.* (1884–5), pp. 4, 9, 25–26.

Swayne.[50] Eventually this problem was solved by Bishop Wordsworth after Dean Hamilton's death. At his visitation in 1888 he announced that he wished to experiment in holding Pentecostal chapters, and asked the dean to summon one annually at least until his next visitation. He also proposed a special annual festival for the commemoration of the cathedral's benefactors on the Tuesday after All Saints which he hoped would give further opportunities for meetings of the whole chapter.[51] Other disagreements within the chapter concerned the choristers' school. Since Canon Hamilton had ceased to direct it, the chapter's policy had been to use the growing revenues from the choristers' fund to increase the number of choristers while discouraging any expansion of the school and forbidding the master to take boarders in addition to the choristers.[52] Bishop Wordsworth, however, established a new school in the close which largely filled the place of the former cathedral grammar school, and in the 20th century the choristers' school has developed into a preparatory school for the public schools.[53]

A more intractable problem was that of the cathedral statutes. Its immensity had been realized by the Cathedral Commissioners of the 1850's, who, like earlier would-be legislators for the cathedral, were dismayed by the mass of obsolete and contradictory medieval statutes and customs. They had recommended an extensive remodelling of the statutes of all the cathedrals of the Old Foundation to make them conform with recent legislation and existing custom.[54] The Commission appointed in 1879 doubted whether it had legal power to make permanent statutes, but by 1884, in co-operation with the dean and chapter, it had prepared a set of draft statutes, consisting of 22 articles, designed to supplement the ancient statutes and customs.[55] The draft statutes, however, were framed on the supposition that the corporation of vicars choral was dissolved. This was not to be done for another half-century, and the draft statutes, although they found favour with bishop, dean, and chapter,[56] never became effective. Chapter acts or ordinances were still made by the close chapter for its own government,[57] but the constitution as a whole remained in many ways unrelated to the statutes.

The most serious problem, however, lay in the chapter's falling income and a long period of increasing financial difficulties, which checked further expansion of the cathedral's work. The communar's accounts for 1878 still showed a surplus of £625 over the chapter's estimated net income of £4,700 a year,[58] but this had vanished by 1885 when the Cathedral Commissioners published their final report. Then they stated that the recent agricultural depression had seriously affected the chapter's income. The position was in fact more serious than it might have been under the old system of small reserved rents and fines; then it took a very great agricultural depression to affect the value of a fine paid for the renewal of a lease, but now the rack rents were immediately affected. The Commission pointed out that the changes made in the period of prosperity had not resulted in benefits to the chapter. The increased revenue from the surrendered lands had gone to the Ecclesiastical Commission, while the chapter was left to deal with the alarming fall in revenue from those which had been returned to it.[59] In 1888 the income of each residentiary was not half of the £500 which had been intended when the estates were transferred.[60] In 1896 an exchange of property was arranged with the Ecclesiastical Commission, but the incomes of dean and canons continued to fall and it was only in 1917 that the Commission eventually agreed to make them up to £1,000 and £500 a year respectively,[61] and by this time the actual value of the money was drastically reduced. A temporary surplus during the following years had to be paid to the Commission by the terms of the 1917 agreement.[62] In 1927 a Cathedral Commission of the Church Assembly declared that the chapter's work was cramped by financial anxiety; the canons' incomes were no longer sufficient to maintain the large canonical houses and expenses of residence in the close, and there had been a big increase in the cost of the cathedral services and fabric.[63] For some time nothing was done. In 1940, however, it was decided to suspend one residentiary canonry and to divide its income among the dean and three remaining residentiaries in order to give the dean £1,200 and the canons £600 a year each.[64] Between 1944 and 1951 the fourth canonry was temporarily restored through the generosity of an anonymous donor.[65] Then the number of residentiary canons returned to three, and the Church Commissioners agreed to make up their incomes to £800 a year each and that of the dean to £1,400,[66] that is, to about the sum suggested as

50 *Salisbury Cath. Com. Rep.* (1884–5), pp. 20, 23–25.

51 *Stat. Sar.* 485, 492–3, 497–9.

52 See article on the school in *V.C.H. Wilts.* v.

53 E. W. Watson, *Life of Bp. Wordsworth*, 200–2; Robertson, *Sarum Close*, 321, 331 sqq.

54 *Cath. Com. 3rd Rep.* pp. ix–x; cf. *1st Rep.* p. xxxvi.

55 *Salisbury Cath. Com. Rep.* (1884–5), pp. 4, 7–11; *Final Rep.* pp. 4–5, 9–10, 14–15.

56 *Salisbury Cath. Com. Rep.* (1884–5), p. 22; *Church Assembly Cath. Com. Rep.* (1927), pp. 7–8, App. p. 323; *Stat. Sar.* 465.

57 *Stat. Sar.* 460–2; *Salisbury Cath. Com. Rep.* (1884–5), p. 4.

58 *Salisbury Cath. Com. Rep.* (1884–5), p. 5.

59 *Cath. Com. Final Rep.* pp. 6–7.

60 *Stat. Sar.* 486.

61 *London Gaz.* p. 3775, Orders in Council, 29 June 1896; p. 5880, 13 June 1917.

62 Sar. Dioc. Regy., Correspondence and Accts. 1920 sqq.

63 *Ch. Assembly Cath. Com. Rep.* (1927), pp. 25–26, 32, 46–47; App. pp. 323, 325–6.

64 Sar. Dioc. Regy., Chapter Min. Bk. 1935–42, f. 313.

65 Ibid. 1943–8, ff. 52–54; 1948–53, 14 Feb. and 1 Apr. 1951.

66 Sar. Dioc. Regy., Correspondence, Nov. 1953.

reasonable for them by the Cathedral Commissioners of 100 years earlier.

THE TWENTIETH CENTURY

Under conditions of increasing financial stringency, and a changing attitude to church attendances, the 20th-century chapter has maintained the work of the cathedral, increased the services, raised the laymen's stipends, reached constitutional decisions, and preserved the cathedral fabric. The influence of Anglo-Catholicism may be seen in the institution in 1915 of a daily communion service, and from 1923 in the wearing of copes by the celebrants for the first time since the Reformation. In 1915 also Sunday evening services were introduced.[67] By 1926 the annual stipends of the six lay vicars had been raised to £115 each, and that of the organist to £330, while three vicars choral had £340 each. By 1952 the organist had £500, the assistant organist £145, and the six lay vicars £968 between them.[68] The vicars choral had been reduced from four to three in 1917, when they had agreed to give part of the fourth vicar's stipend to the choristers' school, which was in financial difficulties.[69] In 1928, however, the chapter sanctioned a scheme for new buildings which allowed the head master to accept boarders in addition to the choristers, and the school again became prosperous and self-supporting.[70] The most pressing constitutional problems were still the continued existence of the corporation of vicars choral and the need for new statutes. With the passage of the Enabling Act of 1919, it seemed possible that the chapter's solutions for these might become law. In 1926 the Cathedral Commissioners heard the representations of Dr. Stanley Baker, procurator of the vicars choral, on behalf of the corporation, and pronounced that he had advanced no strong arguments for its continuance, whereas the bishop and dean and chapter had both urged its dissolution.[71] Finally, under the Cathedrals Measure of 1931, the property of the Salisbury vicars choral was transferred to the dean and chapter in 1934 and the corporation dissolved in 1935, along with minor corporations of other English cathedrals, subject to the rights of existing members. This prepared the way for new statutes which were confirmed by the king in 1937.[72] They provided for not less than two vicars choral to be paid and appointed by the dean and chapter for periods not exceeding ten years in the first instance, with the possibility of reappointment for subsequent periods of not more than five years. Thus the vicars finally lost all the privileges of appointment for life, separate property, and corporate independence, for which their predecessors had fought so hard in the Middle Ages.

These, however, were the biggest changes made in the new statutes, and cannot be described as startling or revolutionary, for they had been advocated by the chapter for over a century and were in any case largely a natural result of the gradual fall in the vicars' numbers since the late 15th century, and of the changed needs of the choir. Other changes illustrate further the adaptation of the cathedral constitution to new needs and conditions, and in most cases merely gave the force of law to practices which had already become customary. The strengthening of the bishop's rights at the cathedral had become desirable when bishops were more often present at their cathedral and when the cathedral was more used for diocesan work. Therefore the bishop was now to have the right, on giving reasonable notice to the dean, to celebrate Holy Communion and to preach in the cathedral when he pleased, and to use any part of the cathedral for synods, visitations, ordinations, confirmations, or other special services; to order the form of these services and to appoint the preachers, so long as the cost did not fall on the chapter's revenues. The dean's greater authority resulted from the reduction in numbers of the cathedral clergy and the greater centralization of the constitution, which again had been proceeding since the Reformation. The new and more exacting rules for canonical residence reflected the more conscientious practice of residence which had developed during the last 60 to 80 years. In future a residentiary canon was forbidden to hold any other benefice with his canonry except with the bishop's consent in writing and was bound to two kinds of annual residence at the cathedral: first his three months' 'close residence', when he was officially 'canon in residence' in charge of the cathedral services; secondly, a further period of five months' 'open residence', when he was to be diligent in attending the services. The rights and privileges of the non-residents, which had been in danger of disappearing altogether, were carefully set out and defined; arrangements were made for paying their expenses when they came to perform their duties at the cathedral; three small prebends had been re-endowed for canons doing religious, educational, or administrative work in the diocese. Phrases or ideas taken from St. Osmund's Institution, Richard Poore's Consuetudinary, and Roger Mortival's Constitutions appeared particularly in the descriptions of the functions and duties of the dignitaries and officers. Moreover, although the new code gave a general view of the whole constitution in 25 chapters logically arranged, it made no claim to completeness. The final paragraph declared that Bishop Osmund's foundation charter and all the ancient statutes and customs were

[67] *Sar. Dioc. Gaz.* li, 100.

[68] *Ch. Assembly Cath. Com. Rep.* (1927), App. p. 324; A. F. Smethhurst, *Salisbury Cathedral: its Finances* (1952), pp. 20–21.

[69] *Ch. Assembly Cath. Com. Rep.* (1927), p. 323; Robertson, *Sarum Close*, 351; Sar. Dioc. Regy., Vicars Choral Box, Procurator's Acct. Bk. 1920–34, f. 1.

[70] Robertson, *Sarum Close*, 532–68.

[71] *Ch. Assembly Cath. Com. Rep.* (1927), App. pp. 322, 324.

[72] *Lond. Gaz.* p. 4898, Orders in Council, 25 July 1934; p. 3216, 4 May 1935; p. 3747, 8 June 1937.

continued and confirmed, unless inconsistent with the present statutes.

The cathedral's history is an impressive witness to the strength of the foundations laid by St. Osmund and his medieval successors. Throughout the centuries the chapter has shown itself capable of astonishing resilience. Periods of apparent decline have been followed by periods of revival, although at no time has the picture of cathedral life been revealed as entirely black or white. Redeeming features have been found in centuries generally looked on as periods of decline, and disappointing ones in those usually described as prosperous and progressive. The strength of the constitution has largely made possible the successive spiritual revivals, by preserving the organization through periods of decline or inertia until better use could be made of it. At all times the constitution has been found capable of adaptation to changing needs and conditions. In 1954 the whole organization is established on a smaller and much less wealthy scale than ever before. The chapter is far less independent of outside control than it has ever been. Probably its biggest contribution to the Church and society was made in the Middle Ages. Yet in recent years, without any adequate financial means of its own, it has successfully achieved costly repairs to the cathedral fabric which have included the preservation of the tower and spire. Voluntary contributions have come in response to its appeals, not merely from the diocese, but from all parts of the country and from overseas; particularly interesting is the support of the Friends of Salisbury Cathedral, the 20th-century organization which has in part taken the place of the medieval confraternity of the chapter.[73]

Deans of Salisbury

Walter, first dean.[74]

? Osbert, obit celebrated 22 Feb.[75]

Robert, died 1111.[76]

Serlo, occurs 1122.[77]

Roger, occurs *c.* 1122–31 to 1139.[78]

Azo, by 1139 until *c.* 1145–8.[79]

Robert, occurs from 1148,[80] consecrated Bp. of Exeter 1155.[81]

Henry de Beaumont, *c.* 1155, consecrated Bp. of Bayeux 1164.[82]

John of Oxford, nominated 1165,[83] election annulled by Pope June 1166,[84] confirmed by Pope Nov. or Dec. 1166,[85] consecrated Bp. of Norwich 1175.[86]

Jordan, occurs from 1176 to *c.* 1193.[87]

Eustace, occurs 1195,[88] consecrated Bp. of Ely 1198.[89]

Richard Poore, S.T.P., made dean 1198,[90] consecrated Bp. of Chichester 1215.[91]

Adam, occurs from 1215, died 1220.[92]

Master William de Wanda, elected 1220,[93] occurs until 1236.[94]

73 Cf. *Ch. Assembly Cath. Com. Rep.* (1927), p. 32, App. p. 325; *W.A.M.* xlviii, 226–7; l, 265; Friends of Salisbury Cath., *Annual Reps.* 1933–54.

74 Lost Martyrology Book of Salisbury quoted by Leland, *Itin.* ed. Toulmin Smith, i, 265.

75 *Fasti Eccl. Sar.* ed. Jones, 308, gives Osbert as Dean of Salisbury *c.* 1102. His only reference, however, is a medieval kalendar of Reading Abbey which says that the obit of 'Osbert, dean' was celebrated on 22 Feb. (B.M. Cott. MS. Vesp. E. 5, f. 12).

76 'Annales de Margan' in *Ann. Mon.* (Rolls Ser.), i, 9.

77 *Reg. St. Osmund* (Rolls Ser.), i, 381, where the charter is wrongly dated *c.* 1108 for 1122: ibid. i, 381–2; W. Farrer, *Itin. Hen. I*, no. 474. 'S. decanus' also occurs in an undated charter of *c.* 1120: *Reg. St. Osmund* (Rolls Ser.), i, 383. He may be the Serlo who became Abbot of Cirencester 1130–1: Florence of Worcester, *Chron.* (Eng. Hist. Soc.), ii, 92, describes Serlo, abbot elect of Cirencester as 'canon of Salisbury'. Leland, quoting the lost Martyrology Book of Salisbury, gives 'Serlo, Decanus Sar' et postea Abbas Cirencestriae': *Itin.* ed. Toulmin Smith, i, 265.

78 In a charter wrongly dated *c.* 1098; *Reg. St. Osmund* (Rolls Ser.), i, 215. For the date: ibid. i, 381–2; W. Farrer, *Itin. Hen. I*, no. 474; *Som. & Dors. N. & Q.* xxiii, 319–20.

79 *Som. & Dors. N. & Q.* xxiii, 319–20; cf. *Reg. St. Osmund* (Rolls Ser.), i, 239, where the date must be *c.* 1142–8, not *c.* 1176 as given. 'Ada decanus', ibid. i, 337, is probably a mistake for Azo.

80 *Sar. Chart. & Doc.* (Rolls Ser.), 14–16, cf. 19; *Reg. St. Osmund* (Rolls Ser.), i, 268–9.

81 R. de Diceto, *Opera Hist.* (Rolls Ser.), i, 301; cf. Gervase of Canterbury, *Hist. Works* (Rolls Ser.), i, 162. There is confusion in the lists of both the bps. of Exeter and deans of Salisbury at this point, Robert of Chichester being given as Dean of Salisbury 1112–38 and as Bp. of Exeter 1138–55; Robert Warelwast as Dean of Salisbury 1139–55 and as Bp. of Exeter from 1155 (*Fasti Eccl. Sar.* ed. Jones, 308; Oliver, *Lives of Bps. of Exeter* (1861), 17, 20). In fact Robert Warelwast was never Dean of Salisbury, but was Bp. of Exeter 1138–55, when he was succeeded by Robert II, Dean of Salisbury, who may possibly have been called Robert of Chichester. This information is owed to Mr. C. N. L. Brooke. The explanation seems to be that at least as early as Godwin's *De Praesulibus Angliae* (1616), 458, a transposition was made between the two Roberts in the list of the bps. of Exeter, and, in moving back one place, Robert II carried his deanery with him; with the result that both Bp. Roberts were then made out to have been deans of Salisbury.

82 *Materials Hist. Becket* (Rolls Ser.), vi, 106; v, 212–15; *Sar. Chart. & Doc.* (Rolls Ser.), 17–18, 35; *Reg. St. Osmund* (Rolls Ser.), i, 218, 228, 337; P. B. Gams, *Series Episcoporum* (1873), p. 506.

83 *Materials Hist. Becket* (Rolls Ser.), iii, 92, 392.

84 Ibid. v, 375, cf. 383, 388, 392–7.

85 Ibid. vi, *passim*; cf. Eyton, *Itin. Hen. II*, 102–3.

86 R. de Diceto, *Opera Hist.* (Rolls Ser.), i, 403.

87 Eyton, *Itin. Hen. II*, 205; *Reg. St. Osmund* (Rolls Ser.), i, 223–4, 241–3, 247, 264, 267, 269; *Sar. Chart. & Doc.* (Rolls Ser.), 42–43, 49; *Stat. Sar.* 38–39; *Pipe R.* 1184–5, 204; *Pipe R.* 1186–7, 187; *Pipe R.* 1187–8, 184 (Pipe R. Soc. xxxiv, xxxvii, xxxviii).

88 Le Neve, *Fasti Eccl. Angl.* ii, 159.

89 R. de Diceto, *Opera Hist.* (Rolls Ser.), ii, 159; R. de Hoveden, *Chron.* (Rolls Ser.), iv, 12, 14; Matthew Paris, *Chron. Maj.* (Rolls Ser.), ii, 446.

90 *Ann. Wint.* in *Ann. Mon.* (Rolls Ser.), ii, 65. *Oxoniensia*, x, 50 n.

91 *Handbk. of British Chronology* (Royal Hist. Soc. 1939), 141.

92 *Sar. Chart. & Doc.* (Rolls Ser.), 78–79; *Reg. St. Osmund* (Rolls Ser.), ii, 15.

93 Ibid. ii, 15–17.

94 *Sar. Chart. & Doc.* (Rolls Ser.), 184, 237.

Master Robert de Hertford, occurs from 1238,[95] died 1257.[96]

Master Robert de Wickhampton, occurs from 1259, elected Bp. of Salisbury 1271.[97]

Master Walter Scammell, elected 1271, but does not occur as dean until after May 1274,[98] consecrated Bp. of Salisbury 1284.[99]

Master Henry de Brandeston, occurs 1285,[1] consecrated Bp. of Salisbury 1287.[2]

Simon de Micham, S.T.P., elected 1287,[3] occurs until 1295.[4]

Peter of Savoy, occurs from 1297 to 1309.[5]

William Rufati, provided 1309.[6]

Reymund de Fargis, called de Got or de la Goth, provided 1311,[7] died by 5 Oct. 1346.[8]

Bertrand de Fargis, provided 1346, died by 26 Feb. 1347.[9]

Master Reynold Orsini (de filiis Ursi, Fitz Urse), provided 1347,[10] died 1374.[11]

James Orsini, D.Can.L., occurs 1374 and 1378,[12] fruits of deanery restored to him after seizure into king's hands, Feb. 1379,[13] died Aug. 1379.[14]

Robert Braybrook, B.C.L., elected 1380,[15] consecrated Bp. of London 1382.[16]

Master Thomas Montagu, Lic.Can.L., Lic.C.L., elected 1382,[17] died 1404.[18]

Master John Chandler, elected 1404,[19] consecrated Bp. of Salisbury 1417.[20]

Simon Sydenham, D.C.L., elected 1418,[21] consecrated Bp. of Chichester 1431.[22]

Thomas Brown, D.C.L., D.Can.L., elected 1431,[23] consecrated Bp. of Rochester 1435.[24]

Master Nicholas Bildeston, elected 1435, died 1441.[25]

Adam Moleyns, D.C.L., elected 1441,[26] consecrated Bp. of Chichester 1446.[27]

Master Richard Leyot, elected 1446, died 1449.[28]

Gilbert Kymer, M.A., B.C.L., M.D., elected 1449,[29] died 1463.[30]

James Goldwell, D.C.L., elected 1463,[31] consecrated Bp. of Norwich 1472.[32]

Master John Davison, elected 1473, died 1485.[33]

Edward Cheyne, D.C.L., D.Can.L., elected 1486, died 1502.[34]

Thomas Ruthall, D.Can.L., elected 1502,[35] consecrated Bp. of Durham 1509.[36]

William Atwater, S.T.P., elected 1509,[37] consecrated Bp. of Lincoln 1514.[38]

John Longland, S.T.P., elected 1514,[39] consecrated Bp. of Lincoln 1521.[40]

Cuthbert Tunstall, D.C.L., elected 1521,[41] consecrated Bp. of London 1522.[42]

Master Richard Pace, elected 1523,[43] died by 20 July 1536.[44]

Master Peter Vannes, occurs from 1536 to 1549.[45]

Master Thomas Cole, said to have been dean temp. Edw. VI.[46]

Master Peter Vannes, occurs again 1552 and 1556,[47] resigned 1563.[48]

95 *Sar. Chart. & Doc.* (Rolls Ser.), 241.

96 Ibid. 330.

97 Ibid. 351–4. He was not consecrated until 1274.

98 Ibid. 352–3; cf. *Cal. Close R.* 1272–9, 117; *Feet of F.* 1272–1327 (W.A.S. Rec. Brch.), 3.

99 *Handbk. Brit. Chronology*, 167.

1 Hist. MSS. Com. *Var. Coll.* i, 344.

2 *Handbk. Brit. Chronology*, 167.

3 Hist. MSS. Com. *Var. Coll.* i, 355.

4 *Sar. Chart. & Doc.* (Rolls Ser.), 367.

5 *Cal. Pat.* 1292–1301, 257; 1307–13, 178.

6 *Reg. S. de Gandavo* (Cant. & York Soc.), 710.

7 Ibid. 760–2.

8 C. Moor, 'Cardinals Beneficed in Sarum Cathedral', *W.A.M.* l, 142.

9 *Cal. Pap. Lett.* 1342–62, 218, 236.

10 *Cal. Pap. Lett.* 1342–62, 236.

11 *W.A.M.* l, 146.

12 Ibid. 146; *Cal. Pap. Lett.* 1362–1404, 196, 227.

13 *Cal. Pat.* 1377–81, 342.

14 *W.A.M.* l, 146.

15 Sar. Reg. Erghum, i, 33*b*; cf. *Cal. Pap. Lett.* 1362–1404, 401.

16 *Handbk. Brit. Chronology*, 159.

17 *Cal. Pap. Lett.* 1362–1404, 401. The Pope provided two cardinals in succession, neither of whom could obtain possession; eventually in 1391 he agreed to Montagu's appointment by way of provision: ibid. 335–6, 401; *Cal. Pat. R.* 1381–5, 237; 1391–6, 566.

18 D. & C. Sar., Reg. Draper, ff. 23–25.

19 Ibid. ff. 74–80.

20 *Handbk. Brit. Chronology*, 167.

21 Sar. Reg. Chandler, pt. ii, 13*b*–16.

22 *Handbk. Brit. Chronology*, 141.

23 Sar. Reg. Neville, pt. ii, 10*b*–13*a*.

24 *Handbk. Brit. Chronology*, 166.

25 Sar. Reg. Neville, pt. ii, 20*b*–23*a*; Reg. Aiscough, pt. ii, 5*a*.

26 Ibid. pt. ii, 5–10; D. & C. Sar., Reg. Houchyns, ff. 135–9.

27 Sar. Reg. Aiscough, pt. ii, 17*b*; *Handbk. Brit. Chronology*, 141.

28 Sar. Reg. Aiscough, pt. ii, 17*b*–18; D. & C. Sar., Reg. Burgh, f. 55.

29 Ibid. ff. 57–58; Sar. Reg. Aiscough, pt. ii, 19.

30 D. & C. Sar., Reg. Newton, f. 58.

31 Ibid. ff. 93–100; Sar. Reg. Beauchamp, i, pt. ii, 66*b*–69.

32 *Handbk. Brit. Chronology*, 161.

33 Sar. Reg. Beauchamp, i, pt. ii, 143–5; Reg. Langton, pt. ii, 7*b*.

34 Ibid. pt. ii, 7*b*–12; Reg. Audley, f. 166*b*.

35 Ibid. ff. 166*b*–8.

36 *Handbk. Brit. Chronology*, 183.

37 D. & C. Sar., Harward's Memorials, f. 127.

38 *Handbk. Brit. Chronology*, 156.

39 D. & C. Sar., Harward's Memorials, ff. 133–4.

40 *Handbk. Brit. Chronology*, 156.

41 D. & C. Sar., Harward's Memorials, f. 35.

42 *Handbk. Brit. Chronology*, 159.

43 D. & C. Sar., Harward's Memorials, f. 40. *Fasti Eccl. Sar.* ed. Jones, 319, and Le Neve, *Fasti Eccl. Angl.* ii, 617, confuse him with Reymund Pade, who was never dean.

44 *L. & P. Hen. VIII*, xi, p. 54. Master Peter Vannes was appointed his coadjutor on account of his infirmities 1535: ibid. x, pp. 417–18. Richard was to be paid an annual pension of £50.

45 Ibid. xi, p. 201; *Cal. Pat.* 1548–9, 424. See also n. 44 above.

46 *Fasti Eccl. Sar.* ed. Jones, 320 n.; Le Neve, *Fasti Eccl. Angl.* ii, 617 n.; *D.N.B.*

47 D. & C. Sar., Reg. Holte and Blacker, f. 62; *Cat. Anct. D.* v, A. 13326.

48 D. & C. Sar., Reg. Blacker, ff. 1, 4.

William Bradbridge, B.D., appointed 1563,[49] consecrated Bp. of Exeter 1571.[50]

Edmund Freke, D.D., appointed 1570,[51] consecrated Bp. of Rochester 1572.[52]

John Piers, D.D., appointed 1572,[53] consecrated Bp. of Rochester 1576, but held deanery *in commendam* until translated to bishopric of Salisbury 1577.[54]

John Bridges, D.D., appointed 1578,[55] consecrated Bp. of Oxford 1604.[56]

John Gordon, D.D., appointed 1604,[57] died 1619.[58]

John Williams, D.D., appointed 1619,[59] appointed Dean of Westminster 1620.[60]

John Bowle, D.D., appointed 1620,[61] consecrated Bp. of Rochester 1630.[62]

Edmund Mason, D.D., appointed 1630,[63] died 1634–5.[64]

Richard Bayley, D.D., appointed 1635,[65] property sequestrated before 1646,[66] restored by 13 Sept. 1660,[67] died 1667.[68]

Ralph Brideoake, D.D., appointed 1667,[69] consecrated Bp. of Chichester 1675.[70]

Thomas Pierce, D.D., appointed 1675,[71] died 1691.[72]

Robert Woodward, D.C.L., appointed 1691,[73] died 1702.[74]

Edward Young, B.C.L., appointed 1702,[75] died 1705.[76]

John Younger, D.D., appointed 1705, died 1728.[77]

John Clarke, D.D., appointed 1728, died 1757.

Thomas Greene, D.D., appointed 1757, died 1780.

Rowney Noel, D.D., appointed 1780, died 1786.

John Eykins, D.D., appointed 1786, died 1808.

Charles Talbot, B.D., appointed 1809, died 1823.

Hugh Nicholas Pearson, D.D., appointed 1823, resigned 1846.

Francis Lear, D.D., appointed 1846, died 1850.

Henry Parr Hamilton, M.A., appointed 1850, died 1880.

George David Boyle, M.A., appointed 1880, died 1901.

Allan Becher Webb, D.D., appointed 1901, died 1907.

William Page Roberts, D.D., appointed 1907, resigned 1919.

Andrew Ewbank Burn, D.D., appointed 1920, died 1927.

John Hugh Granville Randolph, D.D., appointed 1928, resigned 1935.

Edward Lowry Henderson, M.A., appointed 1936, resigned 1943.

Henry Charles Robins, M.A., appointed 1943, resigned 1952.

Robert Hamilton Moberly, M.A., appointed 1952.

The chapter's earliest known seal is the 'old bone seal', which was condemned in 1214.[78] An impression of it, dating probably from Bishop Jocelin's time (1142–84), is in the Cathedral library at Salisbury.[79] It is a pointed oval measuring $2\frac{3}{4} \times 1\frac{7}{8}$ in. It shows the Virgin crowned and seated. Both her arms are raised from the elbow. In her right hand is a fleur-de-lis sceptre. The Child is sitting between her knees. The legend, which is imperfect, reads:

SIG . . . SANCTE MARIE SAR . . . ECCLESIE.

In 1214 the dean and chapter made rules for the use of two common seals:[80]

(1) the greater seal of the dean and chapter, of which several 13th-century impressions survive, including two dating from 1239 and 1266.[81] It is a pointed oval measuring 3×2 in. It shows the Virgin crowned and seated under a plain trefoiled arch with a star over her head. She holds the Child on her

49 Ibid. ff. 2–4; Hist. MSS. Com. *Var. Coll.* i, 371.
50 *Handbk. Brit. Chronology*, 148.
51 D. & C. Sar., Reg. Blacker, ff. 53–56.
52 *Handbk. Brit. Chronology*, 166.
53 D. & C. Sar., Reg. Blacker, ff. 62–64.
54 *Handbk. Brit. Chronology*, 166, 168; Le Neve, *Fasti Eccl. Angl.* ii, 617.
55 D. & C. Sar., Reg. Blacker, ff. 82–84.
56 *Handbk. Brit. Chronology*, 162.
57 D. & C. Sar., Reg. Mortimer, ff. 152–4; cf. *Cal. S.P. Dom.* 1603–10, 104.
58 *Fasti Eccl. Sar.* ed. Jones, 321.
59 Sar. Reg. Fotherby, f. 3.
60 *D.N.B.* s.v. Williams, John.
61 Sar. Reg. Townson, f. 1.
62 *Handbk. Brit. Chronology*, 166.
63 *Cal. S.P. Dom.* 1629–31, 185, 190; Sar. Reg. Davenant, f. 27.
64 *Fasti Eccl. Sar.* ed. Jones, 322.
65 *Cal. S.P. Dom.* 1635, 16; Sar. Reg. Davenant, f. 35.
66 A. G. Matthews, *Walker Revised*, 67.
67 D. & C. Sar., Reg. Greenhill and Butler, f. 1.
68 Le Neve, *Fasti Eccl. Angl.* ii, 618; *Fasti Eccl. Sar.* ed. Jones, 322.
69 *Cal. S.P. Dom. Add.* 1660–85, 210; Ibid. 1667, 339, 353, 390; D. & C. Sar., Reg. Greenhill and Butler, ff. 31*b*–32.
70 *Handbk. Brit. Chronology*, 142.
71 *Cal. S.P. Dom.* 1673–5, 603; 1675–6, 9; D. & C. Sar., Reg. Frome and Prince, ff. 6–9.
72 *D.N.B.*
73 *Cal. S.P. Dom.* 1690–1, 344, 360–1; D. & C. Sar., Reg. Frome and Prince, ff. 117–20.
74 *Fasti Eccl. Sar.* ed. Jones, 324.
75 *Cal. S.P. Dom.* 1700–2, 523, 532; 1702–3, 359; D. & C. Sar., Reg. Frome, ff. 5–12.
76 *Fasti Eccl. Sar.* ed. Jones, 324.
77 From 1705 to 1880 the list of deans has been taken from *Fasti Eccl. Sar.* ed. Jones, 324–5 and Le Neve, *Fasti Eccl. Angl.* ii, 618–19; from 1880 to 1954 from the list in Sar. Dioc. Regy.
78 *Stat. Sar.* pp. 40–41. Its use in the late 12th century is mentioned: *Reg. St. Osmund* (Rolls Ser.), i, 299, 303.
79 In showcase.
80 *Stat. Sar.* pp. 40–43.
81 B.M. Add. Ch. 19620; xxxvii, 78; lviii, 60. DL 27/10; E 42/377. Illustrated in Hoare, *Mod. Wilts.* City of Salisbury, plate i, no. 1.

left knee and He is reaching up towards the fleur-de-lis sceptre which she holds in her right hand. The perfect legend, as shown by the several impressions together, is:

SIGILL' · SANCTE · MARIE · SARESB'IENSIS · ECCL'IE

The seal of Adam [de Esseby], the chancellor, was used as a counter seal to this seal in 1239.[82] It is a pointed oval measuring $1\frac{7}{8} \times 1\frac{3}{8}$ in., and shows the chancellor sitting on a high-backed chair under a trefoiled and pinnacled canopy and on a foliated bracket. He is reading a book lying on a lectern before him. The legend reads:

SIGILL : ADE : CANCELLARII : SAR'

(2) the lesser seal *ad citaciones*.[83] Probably this was the seal *ad peticiones et ad causas*, of which several impressions survive from the 13th century and later.[84] The bronze gilt matrix was in use up to 1936. This seal is practically the same shape and size as the chapter's greater seal, being only slightly narrower: $3 \times 1\frac{7}{8}$ in. The subject is the same, but more elaborately executed: the crowned Virgin, with the Child on her left knee, sits on a carved throne, from which spring the slender shafts of a trefoiled canopy with seven pinnacles. The bracket beneath is deeply carved. On one side of the Virgin's head is a new moon and on the other a star. The legend reads:

S' · $\overline{\text{SCE}}$ · MARIE · SARESBIRIENSIS · $\overline{\text{ECCE}}$ · AD · PETICIONES · ET · AD · $\overline{\text{CAS}}$ ·

The common seal of the vicars choral dates probably from the 13th century.[85] It is a pointed oval, measuring $2\frac{1}{8} \times 1\frac{9}{16}$ in. It shows the coronation of the Virgin. The corbel in the base, on which the two figures are supported, is ornamented with an elegant flower. The legend reads:

S' COMMUNE VIC'RIOR' ECCL'E SARESBIRIENS'[86]

Other seals in the British Museum or Cathedral library include the seal of an unidentified 14th-century dean, an early 15th-century seal of the office of dean, a 17th-century seal of the officiality of the decanal jurisdiction, a 17th-century seal of the communar of the dean and chapter, and several seals of the prebendal jurisdictions and of individual dignitaries and prebendaries.

[82] B.M. Add. Ch. 19620; DL 27/10. Illustrated in Hoare, op. cit. plate i, no. 9.

[83] *Stat. Sar.* pp. 42–43.

[84] C 148/18; H.O. 44/30; B.M. l, 21; lviii, 61; Salisbury Cathedral libr. showcase. Two impressions can be dated 1286 and 1837. Illustrated in Hoare, op. cit. plate i, no. 2.

[85] B.M. D.C., E. 192; Salisbury Cathedral libr. Illustrated in Hoare, op. cit. plate i, no. 11.

[86] Described in Birch, *Cat. of Seals in B.M.* i, 346–9.

LIST OF CLASSES OF PUBLIC RECORDS

USED IN THIS VOLUME, WITH THEIR CLASS NUMBERS

Chancery
- C 1 Proceedings, Early
- C 47 Miscellanea
- C 60 Fine Rolls
- C 66 Patent Rolls
- C 76 Treaty Rolls
- C 81 Warrants for the Great Seal, Series I
- C 136 Inquisitions post mortem Rich. II
- C 142 Inquisitions post mortem Series II
- C 143 Inquisitions ad quod damnum
- C 146 Ancient Deeds, Series C
- C 147 „ „ „ CC
- C 148 „ „ „ CS

Court of Common Pleas
- CP 25 Feet of Fines
- CP 25(1) „ „ Series I

Exchequer of Receipt
- E 401 Receipt Rolls

Exchequer, Treasury of Receipt
- E 32 Forest Proceedings
- E 36 Miscellaneous Books
- E 40 Ancient Deeds, Series A
- E 41 „ „ „ AA
- E 42 „ „ „ AS

Exchequer, Queen's Remembrancer
- E 101 Accounts, Various
- E 106 Extents of Alien Priories
- E 135 Ecclesiastical Documents
- E 164 Miscellaneous Books, Series I
- E 179 Subsidy Rolls, &c.
- E 210 Ancient Deeds, Series D
- E 212 „ „ „ DS
- E 213 „ „ „ RS

Exchequer, Augmentation Office
- E 301 Certificates of Chantries and Colleges
- E 305 Deeds of Purchase and Exchange
- E 314 Miscellanea
- E 315 Miscellaneous Books
- E 318 Particulars for Grants of Crown Land
- E 322 Surrenders of the Monasteries
- E 323 Treasurer's Accounts
- E 326 Ancient Deeds, Series B
- E 327 „ „ „ BX
- E 329 „ „ „ BS

Exchequer, First Fruits and Tenths
- E 331 Institutions, Bishops' Certificates
- E 334 Composition Books

Exchequer, Lord Treasurer's Remembrancer
- E 359 Enrolled Accounts, Subsidies
- E 368 Memoranda Rolls
- E 372 Pipe Rolls
- E 377 Recusant Rolls

Home Office
- HO 44 Correspondence, George IV and later
- HO 129 Various, Census, Ecclesiastical Returns

Justices Itinerant
- Just. Itin.1 Assize Rolls, Eyre Rolls, &c.
- Just. Itin.3 Gaol Delivery Rolls

Clerks of Assize
- Assizes 24 Miscellaneous Books, Western Circuit

Court of Queen's Bench
- KB 9 Ancient Indictments
- KB 27 Coram Rege Rolls
- KB 138 Writs and Returns

Duchy of Lancaster
- DL 5 Decrees and Orders, Entry Books
- DL 7 Inquisitions post mortem
- DL 27 Deeds, Series LS
- DL 29 Ministers' Accounts
- DL 30 Court Rolls
- DL 40 Knights' Fees, Returns
- DL 41 Miscellanea
- DL 42 Miscellaneous Books

Special Collections
- SC 1 Ancient Correspondence
- SC 6 Ministers' Accounts
- SC 7 Papal Bulls
- SC 8 Ancient Petitions
- SC 12 Rentals and Surveys, Portfolios
- SC 13 Seals

State Paper Office
- SP 16 State Papers Domestic, Chas. I
- SP 29 State Papers, Chas. II

Court of Wards and Liveries
- Wards 2 Deeds and Evidences

NOTE ON ABBREVIATIONS

Among the abbreviations and short titles used, the following, which occur frequently throughout the volume, may require elucidation. Documents forming part of the muniments of the City of Salisbury and Borough of Wilton are cited by the references assigned to them by the editor of the *List of Wiltshire Borough Records earlier in date than 1836* (W.A.S. Rec. Brch. v).

D. & C. Sar.	Dean and Chapter of Salisbury
Sar. Dioc. Regy*	Diocesan Registry, Salisbury
W.A.S.	Wiltshire Archaeological and Natural History Society
W.A.S. Libr., Devizes	Library of W.A.S. in the Museum, Devizes
W.A.S. Rec. Brch.	Records Branch of W.A.S.
W.R.O.	Wiltshire Record Office, Trowbridge
Antrobus D. (W.A.S. Rec. Brch.)	Pugh, R. B. (ed.) *Calendar of Antrobus Deeds before 1625* (W.A.S. Rec. Brch. iii)
Aubrey, *Topog. Coll.* ed. Jackson	Jackson, J. G. (ed.) *Topographical Collections of John Aubrey* (W.A.S. Devizes, 1862)
Cal. Feet of F. Wilts. 1195–1272, ed. Fry	Fry, E. A. (ed.) *Calendar of Feet of Fines Wilts.* 1195–1272 (W.A.S. Devizes, 1930)
Cart. Sax. ed. Birch	Birch, W. de Gray (ed.) *Cartularium Saxonicum*
Cod. Dipl. ed. Kemble	Kemble, J. M. (ed.) *Codex Diplomaticus Aevi Saxonici*
Crockford	Crockford's *Clerical Directory*
Dugd. *Mon.*	Dugdale, W. *Monasticon Anglicanum* (edn. 1817–30)
Fasti Eccl. Sar. ed. Jones	Jones, W. H. *Fasti Ecclesiae Sarisberiensis* (Salisbury and London, 1879)
Feet of F. Wilts. 1272–1327 (W.A.S. Rec. Brch.)	Pugh, R. B. (ed.) *Abstracts of Feet of Fines Wilts for reigns of Edw. I and Edw. II* (W.A.S. Rec. Brch. i).
Hoare, *Mod. Wilts.*	Hoare, Sir R. Colt. *Modern Wiltshire.* (1822–37)
Leland, *Itin.* ed. Toulmin Smith	Leland, J. *Itinerary*, &c., ed. Lucy Toulmin Smith
Phillipps, *Wilts. Inst.*	Phillipps, Sir Thomas (ed.) *Institutiones Clericorum in Comitatu Wiltoniae* (Priv. printed 1825)
Reg. Simon de Gandavo (Cant. & York Soc.)	Flower, C. T., and Dawes, M. C. B. (ed.) *Registrum Simonis de Gandavo* (Canterbury and York Society)
W.A.M.	*Wiltshire Archaeological and Natural History Magazine*
W.N. & Q.	*Wiltshire Notes and Queries*
Wilts. Inq. p.m. 1242–1326 (Index Libr.)	Fry, E. A. (ed.) *Abstracts of Wilts. Inq. p.m.* 1242–1326 (Index Library, xxxvii)
Wilts. Inq. p.m. 1327–77 (Index Libr.)	Stokes, Ethel (ed.) *Abstracts of Wilts. Inq. p.m.* 1327–77 (Index Library, xlviii)

* Among the abbreviations used for citing records in the Diocesan Registry are the following:

Ep. Citations	Citations to Consistory Court
Ep. Lib. Act.	Consistory Court Act Books
Ep. Lib. Dep.	Consistory Court Deposition Books
Ep. Lib. Vis.	Visitation Books
Ep. Vis. Chw. Pres.	Churchwardens' Presentments made in episcopal visitations
Archd. Sarum, Archd. Wilts, Dec., Subdec.	Act Books and Deposition Books of Archdeacons of Sarum and Wilts and of Dean and Subdean

THE VICTORIA HISTORY OF THE COUNTIES OF ENGLAND

WILTSHIRE

The History of Wiltshire, from which the Salisbury Cathedral section has been reprinted, is a major work of reference on local history, based on original research and achieving a high standard of scholarship. The compilation of the Wiltshire volumes is sponsored jointly by Wiltshire County Council, Thamesdown District Council and the other four district councils in the county. It is being carried out by a small team of experts led by Dr. D. A. Crowley. The volumes so far published are listed below.

I	Part one. Physique of Wiltshire; archaeological gazetteer, 1957. 279 pages
I	Part two. Prehistory, 1973. 219 pages, including index to Parts 1 and 2. 0 19 722735 x
II	Anglo-Saxon Wiltshire, Anglo-Saxon Art, Domesday, and Geld Rolls, 1955. 245 pages
III	Ecclesiastical history, 1956. 424 pages
IV	Economic history, 1959. 486 pages
V	Administrative and political history, 1957. 383 pages
VI	Wilton, Salisbury, and Underditch hundred, 1962 reprinted 1984. 239 pages. 0 7129 1032 8
VII	Bradford, Melksham, and Potterne and Cannings hundreds, 1953 reprinted 1985. 241 pages. 0 7129 1036 0
VIII	Warminster, Westbury, and Whorwellsdown hundreds, 1965. 285 pages. 0 19 722710 4
IX	Kingsbridge hundred, including Swindon, 1970. 220 pages. 0 19 722736 8
X	Swanborough hundred and Devizes, 1975. 347 pages. 0 19 722740 6
XI	Downton and Elstub and Everleigh hundreds, 1980. 284 pages. 0 19 722751 1
XII	Ramsbury and Selkley hundreds and Marlborough, 1983. 257 pages. 0 19 722759 7
XIII	Chalke and Dunworth hundreds. *In progress*
—	A history of Swindon to 1965 reprinted from Volume IX, 1983. 80 pages. 0 86080 107 1

Volumes less than three years old are distributed by Oxford University Press and older ones by Wm. Dawson & Sons Ltd. The reprint of *A history of Swindon to 1965* is uniform with this volume and is distributed by Wiltshire County Council Library & Museum Service.